THE COMING
POLITICAL BREAKTHROUGH

The two parties which divide the state, the party of Conservatism and that of Innovation, are very old. Now one, now the other wins the day, and still the fight renews itself as if for the first time. It is the opposition of Past and Future, of Memory and Hope.

RALPH WALDO EMERSON
December 9th, 1841

The Coming
Political Breakthrough

CHESTER BOWLES

THE BODLEY HEAD
LONDON

© Chester Bowles 1959
Printed and bound in Great Britain for
THE BODLEY HEAD LTD
10 Earlham Street, London, WC2
by Staples Printers Ltd, Rochester, Kent
Set in Intertype Baskerville

First published in Great Britain 1960

To
Barbara, Ches, Cynthia,
Sarah and Sam

Contents

[continued over

Foreword

EMERSON once suggested that the most meaningful differences in American life have occurred when the advocates of a Party of Hope clashed with those of a Party of Memory.

It must be added that for extended periods both of our formal political organizations have appeared all too content with their own memories and the slogans and attitudes associated with them.

Yet at a critical juncture, one or the other has managed to break through the clichés and the commonplace, and for brief, creative interludes, has emerged as the Party of Hope to recall America to greatness.

The result has been a kind of rhythm in American political history which has been noted by several observers. In the spring of 1956 I added my own views in a little book entitled, *American Politics in a Revolutionary World,* based on the Godkin Lectures which I had recently given at Harvard.

In this book I sought to identify and describe our periods of national apathy and ineffectiveness and the surges of political creativeness that followed them.

I suggested that after the tension-packed 1930's and 1940's a period of breath-catching had been inevitable, but that this period was gradually running its course, and that the stage might soon be set for a fresh and more affirmative approach to domestic and international problems.

Yet political readjustments usually take place slowly. Practical experience has taught political leaders that familiar election-year appeals are the safest.

Therefore I doubted that the new national consensus on domestic and foreign policy matters which I believe has been taking shape, would greatly affect what was said or done in the election campaign that lay just ahead.

This turned out to be the case.

9

The Republicans, entrenched behind an extraordinarily popular leader, saw no compelling need to define their objectives or their means of reaching them.

It was enough for them to attack the Democrats as spenders and warmongers, and to point confidently to President Eisenhower as the symbol of peace and prosperity.

Democratic political strategists were likewise persuaded that the public was not yet ready for new issues, and that the familiar bread-and-butter appeals were still the prescription of victory.

A brilliant new period of political creativeness, they agreed, might indeed be right around the corner. But didn't the record show that traditionally we had backed into such periods cautiously and without fanfare?

In his first inaugural on the eve of the Civil War had not Lincoln said that he had no legal right to free the slaves?

In the depths of the Great Depression had not Roosevelt promised to balance the budget by reducing the cost of 'Federal Government operations' by twenty-five per cent?

The wisest course, therefore, was again to key the Democratic appeal to the farm, labour and small business groups which had been mobilized to provide successive Presidential victories from 1932 to 1948.

In Adlai Stevenson the Democrats had one of the most knowledgeable and eloquent spokesmen of our century. No one living could have stood with greater conviction and integrity for the new political consensus which was waiting to be born.

But the stage was unprepared. Democratic councils were divided. The opportunity for the party as a whole to focus public debate on the central issues slipped by.

With the Democrats tactically divided on what the debate should be about and with the Republicans feeling no necessity to debate at all, the political breakthrough predictably failed to develop.

Indeed, the radiant good will emanating from the personality of the President was such that the outcome of the election was never in doubt. In retrospect, it may fairly be said that the Democrats would have lost regardless of what they said.

Four years have passed. Once more we stand on the eve of a Presidential election.

There is nothing novel about describing an impending election as the most important ever held. We all admire courage, and the claim that we are about to tackle problems which dwarf those our fathers faced makes heroes of us all.

Yet this time the claim is a valid one.

The 1960 election falls at a strategic moment. If our two parties again fail to come to grips with the enormous questions now crowding in upon us, the likelihood of another national resurgence will fade. Indeed, a wrong course of action or continued confusion in the next four years can lead straight to a general calamity.

It is from the deeply felt conviction that 1960 may be the decisive election of our century that I have written this book.

Since it deals with politics, I hope no one will expect me to hide my political feelings. As a former Democratic Governor and a current Democratic Congressman, my party allegiance can scarcely be disguised.

Twenty years of active participation in Democratic party affairs have inevitably given me my own perspective. I am confident it will be judged against others, and that appropriate allowances will be made.

CHESTER BOWLES

Washington, DC
September 1959

PART I

Rediscovering
our National Purpose

What constitutes the bulwark of our own liberty and independence? It is not our frowning battlements or our bristling sea coasts. . . . Our reliance is in the love of liberty which God has planted in us. Our defence is in the spirit which prized liberty as the heritage of all men, in all lands everywhere.

ABRAHAM LINCOLN
Edwardsville, Illinois, September 13th, 1858

CHAPTER I

Prelude to a Great Decision

IN THE four years that have passed since the 1956 Presidential election, millions of thoughtful Americans have experienced a mounting unease.

As they contrast the scope of the world-wide challenge with the inadequacy of our response, they wonder if our years of greatness may not be numbered.

William Faulkner, our Nobel Prize winner for literature, spoke for this mood when he recently asked : 'What has happened to the American Dream?' He answered in part : 'We dozed, slept, and it abandoned us.

'There no longer sounds a unifying voice speaking our mutual hope and will,' he continued. Instead, what we now hear 'is a cacophony of terror and conciliation and compromise, babbling only the mouth sounds, the loud and empty words – "freedom, democracy, patriotism" – from which we have emasculated all meaning whatever.'

Although most Americans feel, as I do, that such pessimism is extreme, it would be folly to underestimate what is now required of us. We are in fact confronted with a totally new set of problems which are breathtaking in their variety and explosiveness.

1. In Asia, Africa and Latin America 800 million newly free or soon to be free people are straining to create new societies or to shore up the foundations of old ones.

Their excited new awareness of what modern technology can do has generated expectations which cannot possibly be met with existing technical and capital resources.

At the same time the economic gap between the rich minority, living largely in North America and Western Europe, and the poor majority, living largely in Africa, Asia and Latin America, continues to grow.

'The West likes to think and speak of the Atlantic community as the heart of the free world,' said the Burmese delegate to the United Nations in April 1959, 'but to most of the earth's population, it seems less the free world than just the rich world.

'What is more disturbing from the point of view of the West is that all the current trends show it becoming a smaller and smaller minority getting relatively richer and richer.

'The prosperous Atlantic countries today are in a position resembling that of the aristocrats of the eighteenth century. They had served a useful purpose, but new and powerful classes were swelling up below them.

'Some aristocrats, like the French, met the challenge head on, and perished. Some, like the British, found they had much in common with their rivals and so survived, first as leaders and later as equal partners.'

The Burmese delegate could have added a further element to his comparison : the embittering fact that the richer Atlantic peoples happen to be largely white, while the poorer Asians, Africans and Latin Americans are largely coloured.

2. In the meantime, the Soviet Union has suddenly emerged from a peasant society to become a mighty industrial complex that now challenges the economic and political position of the United States.

The architects of Russia's industrialization have often seemed to consider every lie a higher truth, every cruelty a higher kindness, every treachery a higher faithfulness.

But, they assert, the accomplishments of Soviet technology ultimately will justify Soviet methods in the eyes of the world. The rate of Soviet economic expansion, they point out, is already four times our own, while Soviet universities are turning out twice as many scientists and engineers.

History has not yet rendered a final judgment on the Soviet experiment. Yet the extraordinary material forces which are being generated in the Soviet Union, combined with the

Marxist faith in the inevitability of success, add up to a formidable challenge.

3. Similar deep-seated international divisions between opposing power blocs are as old as history. But now there is a difference : each side is armed to the teeth with nuclear weapons that could destroy most of civilization.

As a surging military technology provides the two rivals with ever more destructive weapons, there is an awesome danger that a failure in communications or a human error on either side may lead to nuclear catastrophe.

4. Complicating this sombre global sketch still further is the new China. The iron-fisted Communist dictatorship in Peking, allied with Moscow and deeply antagonistic to us, is hammering 650 million able, hard-working human beings into a new centre of Communist strength with an incredible power potential.

The inadequacy of China's natural resources in relation to her vast population suggests an effort at some future time to occupy the areas to the south.

5. If America's domestic house were in good order, the challenge we face on so many world fronts would be profound. But our house is not in good order.

We have just emerged from our third recession in ten years. Since 1953 our economy has been growing at the slowest rate in generations, scarcely enough to meet our increasing population needs.

In the meantime our educational needs intensify. The number of new homes built each year barely equals the number of old homes condemned each year as slums. Hospital building and medical research lag behind our needs. Our transportation system is inadequate. Much of our industrial plant is obsolescent.

6. Finally, in our inventory of things amiss in our national house, we come to the question of civil rights. Nearly a hundred years after the Emancipation Proclamation, Negro Americans in some states are still denied the right to vote and

to secure an equal public education. In almost every state they are denied equal rights in housing and employment.

Faced with these harsh domestic and international realities, our national leadership has given no sign that it recognizes the magnitude of our task. On the contrary it continues to act on the comfortable, standstill assumptions that have traditionally characterized the Party of Memory.

Its response to the Soviet challenge has vacillated between reckless brinkmanship and diplomatic naïveté. Its response to China has fluctuated between indifference and belligerence.

Its response to our slow rate of economic growth has been to revert to the scarcity view that inflation can only be checked by leaving idle a substantial portion of our men, machines and capital. Its response to our need for more schools, housing and hospitals is to tell us that adequate facilities are beyond our means.

Its response to the greatest moral crisis of our time, racial discrimination, has been almost exclusively legalistic.

Admittedly no generation of Americans has faced simultaneously so many challenges of so many kinds on so many sides. But the fact remains that we have not been measuring up.

In times past, and in very real ways, we were the giver of light in a sorely troubled world. We are not lacking in the capacity to continue in that role.

Far from it. Our enormous untapped material and human resources make it possible for us to play an even more important role in the future. The world yearns for us to apply the force of our tested. democratic values to the solution of evolving new problems.

What we do with the opportunity depends in large part on the individual whom we elect to the Presidency in November 1960. But it also depends on the character of the campaign debate and the basis on which we make our choice.

The Presidency is the central place of action in our national life. It is the one focal point which gives unity, direction and purpose to the American people as a whole. This fact must be uppermost in our minds when we choose a President in 1960.

Closely related to it is the fact that whoever proves to be the victor in 1960, he and his party will have but a few effective years in which to accomplish their main work. Every twentieth-century President who has accomplished anything new did most of it during the first three years of his Administration.

In each case the period that followed was marked by a resurgence in the opposition's power to block further advances, by distracting issues arising over personalities and bids for a second term, or by the struggle over the Presidential succession.

If the new President whom we choose in 1960 can expect no more than three years in which to break new ground, it is essential that we consider beforehand what we want his new Administration to do.

The more we talk about it, the more likely it is that our talk will work its way into the bloodstream of the two political parties. It will help determine the sort of candidates they choose, the character of the contest between them, the election outcome in November 1960, and the political framework within which the new President chooses his cabinet, charts his course, and proposes his programme of action.

This brings us to the relationship between the rank and file of American voters and the political activists who constitute the professional managers and the party workers.

It has long been fashionable in America to denounce politics and politicians indiscriminately. Yet it is worth noting that only through politics can we define, advance, test and decide whether this or that proposal can best serve the common interest.

Only through politics can men who hold the trust of public office be made to explain their actions, and be held accountable for the way they use their power.

Only through politics can public opinion make its presence felt as a controlling, disciplining and guiding force in the operations of a democratic government.

Which is to say that only by keeping our political system in good working order can we, as a democratic people, march at the head of events, and by taking measures born of fore-sight, *produce* the events we want, instead of waiting for events produced by others to overtake us willy-nilly.

Indeed, any American who says that he "stands above politics" comes close to saying that he stands outside our American democratic society.

At the opposite pole are those millions of conscientious citizens who have a vague sense of guilt because they are not more fully engaged in politics.

They have been told that both political parties urgently need workers. Yet their time and energies are subject to many other pressing and legitimate claims – the claims of family, children and the simple economics of living.

In addition there are the human uncertainties which bear down on the thoughts of any man who, as a novice, is asked to enter a new and complex field of activity.

We may earnestly hope that the number of direct political participants in both parties will grow steadily larger. Yet it would be unrealistic to expect anything like a majority of the American people to become active party workers.

What, then, can they do that is both useful and within the realm of the possible? Is there a middle ground between a total rejection of politics on the one side and a nearly full-time career as a political activist on the other?

I believe that there is. The thoughtful citizen can go far to discharge his political responsibilities to his community, state and nation by becoming adequately informed and by bringing his knowledge to bear in several direct and indirect ways.

He can develop a broad and perceptive awareness of his long-term self-interest as a member of both the American and world community.

He can insist that the level of politics be raised beyond narrow and confining interests to planes of action more consistent with this larger vision of America's role.

He can help reaffirm the validity of the basic ideas which underlie our whole democratic faith and which have lately become tarnished through misappropriation or neglect.

He can let the professional politician know in unmistakable terms what course of action he favours in dealing with domestic and foreign problems.

He can learn intelligently to appraise the quality and effectiveness of the professionals whom he elects to office, and to call them to account for the consequences of what they do or fail to do.

As we move toward the decisive election of 1960, what then should we as citizens want and expect our political representatives to do for us? How can we prod them into more effective action?

CHAPTER II

A Theory of Political Growth

AMERICAN politics operate within the framework of a broadly accepted code of conduct. As our major parties shift from a dominant to a minority status within that framework they follow surprisingly consistent patterns.

I do not have in mind short-run political ups-and-downs where a politically attractive personality can temporarily give the advantage to one or the other party. Rather I refer to the stirrings which reflect deeper convictions and a changing emphasis in our national perspective.

Because they have a direct bearing on the dangers and opportunities facing the Republican and Democratic parties alike as they prepare for the 1960 contest, let me briefly try to retrace those shifting patterns and to identify their characteristics.

As I see our American political tradition, a minority party begins to move to a majority status when two lines of force begin to converge. First, the more alert leaders and members of that party sense that new problems are developing to which old political answers are inadequate. Second, and relatedly, they sense that the people are ready to support the party which offers an affirmative and realistic new response.

Then follows a period of debate and manoeuvre within the party circle during which these leaders win the ascendancy. Through their speeches and legislative efforts they gradually establish their party in the public mind as the vehicle through which the new challenge can most effectively be met. Simultaneously they bring together a coalition of economic and political interests which generally subscribe to the new public consensus. Gradually the stage is set for a political breakthrough on a national scale.

In the course of this evolving process, the issues between the older and the newer views are sometimes debated fully, and the voters are given a clearly stated choice between alternatives. At other times we have backed into a new political era under pressure from a national crisis while clinging to a folklore and to slogans that had lost their relevance.

The party representing the new consensus may deliberately chart its course, as in the days of Jefferson. Or it may find itself caught up by forces which direct its actions after the election is won, as in the cases of Lincoln and Franklin Roosevelt.

In either event it has temporarily made itself the Party of Hope. Its social and economic inventiveness is rewarded by successive victories at the polls despite the opposition of the Party of Memory, which clings to old issues and old habits of mind.

Ultimately, however, the minority party produces leaders who begin to see that for better or for worse the new ways have come to stay. They understand that as long as their party resists the changes which have taken place and which now have general public support, it will have nothing to look forward to except further defeats in national elections.

Thus they begin to embrace the measures advanced by the majority, while seeking to reaffirm their own political identity through promises to handle those measures with greater effectiveness, honesty or political finesse. The last twelve years, it seems to me, comprise such a period.

But a political line drawn on such a basis is as difficult to maintain as a line drawn through water. What generally ensues instead is a mark-time period of apathy and boredom among the voters as the stated differences between the parties diminish. Political personalities become more important than issues, and the election-day fortunes of the two parties alternate accordingly.

Eventually, however, a critical domestic or international situation develops which demands a new approach. The opposition party, more sensitive to the new challenge, confronts the incumbents with a coalition of national forces expressive of a new consensus and powerful enough to bring about a sweeping political breakthrough.

The cycle then repeats itself as the new dominant party, firmly based on the new national consensus, has its chance to write history.

In all of this, the periods of ascendancy and defeat can vary widely in duration. Moreover, the lines between them may often be ill-defined. Yet a study of American history reveals a remarkable consistency in the character of the cycles to which I have referred.

From the birth of our political parties to the present, three such great eras of consensus are discernible.

Each developed in response to public insistence on a broader interpretation of human freedom to meet new conditions. Each was characterized in its early stages by great political

creativeness and bitter debates, followed by a period of adjustment and climaxed by an 'era of good feeling' as we rested
from our creative exertions and recharged our national
batteries.

The first era, largely dominated by the Democratic party,
extended from Jefferson's victory in 1800 to the outbreak of
the Civil War in 1861. It was characterized by the broad
public acceptance for the first time in history of a system of
government closely responsive to the majority will.

To be sure, Alexander Hamilton and his opposition
Federalists pioneered the structural mechanics of a federal
government *for* the people. And for this durable achievement
a great debt is owed to them.

Yet in Hamilton's view government decisions were to be
entrusted to the 'well-bred and the well-born'. In contrast, the
democratic faith of Jefferson and Jackson called for government *of* and *by* the people as well.

By the 1840's and the 1850's this question had been basically
settled and a new issue, slavery, was steadily pressing to the
centre of the political stage. Both the Whigs – conservative in
their definition of the Jeffersonian issues – and the more
liberal Democrats were keenly aware that this embittering new
question would split their forces up the middle. Both attempted
to ignore and submerge it.

Yet because slavery was the central issue in the public mind,
it persisted in forcing itself into the arena of political action.
Inevitably the demand grew for a new and more effective
political vehicles with which to cope with it. In 1856 my
grandfather, Samuel Bowles, editor of the Springfield *Republican,* voiced this demand in the following sweeping terms :

> Old party names must be forgotten, old party ties sur-
> rendered, organization based on secondary issues abandoned,
> momentary self-interest sacrificed to the country and its
> welfare, and all must stand together and fight and labour
> side by side until the great question which overshadows all
> others has found issue in the triumph of justice.

The subsequent election in 1860 of our first Republican President, Abraham Lincoln, established the political dominance of a new consensus which continued in American public affairs for seventy years.

This new consensus imposed on the democratic inheritance of the Jeffersonian–Jacksonian consensus a fresh American response to the Industrial Revolution. It included a broadening of civil rights, the expansion of the nation's human resources through immigration from Europe, the settlement of the West, high tariffs, and the large-scale development of an old instrument – the corporation – to assemble money, materials, machines and men for the accelerated economic development of the nation.

The Republican party, which largely dominated this consensus, lost decisively in 1932 because it no longer appeared responsive to the unprecedented new challenge to economic security and human dignity presented by the Great Depression.

The period of the third consensus was ushered in by Mr Roosevelt and carried forward by Mr Truman. It reflected a far broader acceptance by our government of direct responsibility for minimum standards of living and opportunity and for more direct American participation in world affairs.

Although the public demonstrated the strength of this consensus by electing a Democratic President in five successive elections, it was a time of crisis at home and abroad and bitter partisan debates on how best to cope with them. In 1952 most Americans were eager for an opportunity to catch their political breath and to turn away from divisive domestic and international questions.

Under pressure of rapidly broadening domestic and global challenges which we briefly considered in the first chapter, I believe that we are now moving into a fourth period of political creativeness which will be dominated by a new consensus evolving logically out of the third.

This new consensus will reaffirm and broaden our commit-

ment to sustained full employment without inflation and
without sharp recessions. It will call for a more realistic,
nationwide approach to civil rights. It will encourage an
improvement in the *quality* of our day-to-day living. And it
will bring our relations with the world into a fresh perspective,
which may enable us to act more affirmatively.

If I am correct in this appraisal, the prospect ahead of us
is this : the political leadership of America in 1960 will be
entrusted to the party which most boldly and effectively
identifies itself with this fourth consensus, and casts up leaders
and programmes of action consistent with it. This party will
continue as the dominant party until the objectives of the
new consensus have been achieved and its vitality finally spent.

This means that the interests of the people as a whole and
the enlightened self-interest of our two political parties now
coincide. If one or the other succeeds as the Party of Hope in
making itself the *action instrument* of that fourth consensus,
the public interest will be the gainer and the party, itself, will
be the winner.

In the chapter that follows, I shall relate the new fourth
consensus to the larger theme of our national purpose – a
topic which merits, I believe, our most urgent consideration.

CHAPTER III

What Is Our National Purpose ?

THE political breakthrough which may be just ahead involves,
and may in fact depend upon, our ability to clarify our
national purpose in terms of recent critical developments both
at home and abroad.

What is our national purpose?

The question would be provocative at any time. But now,

in the form of the Soviet Union we are faced with a determined and effective challenger who tells us bluntly that we
embody an antiquated order of values and that the future
belongs to Communism.

Goodwill missions, high-level exchanges, and summit meet-
ings may be useful in creating a more pleasant atmosphere.
But they should not blind us to the challenge itself.

It is sheer folly to ignore the power of the Communist
appeal to frustrated, impoverished people who are searching
for some decisive short cut to grow more food, to build schools,
health clinics, roads, and to achieve a new sense of individual
belonging in our complex, high-pressured world.

Even in the recurrent periods when Radio Moscow mutes
its direct attacks on the United States, it continues around the
clock to speak the magic words of social and political revolution to the people of Asia, Africa and South America.

In a hundred languages these restless millions are told that
the Soviet Union alone among the great powers supports
colonial struggles for independence, that alone it backs the
dark-skinned majority of the human race against discrimination by the white minority, and that it is eager and ready to
provide science, technology and capital for their more rapid
economic development.

Simultaneously the Kremlin works to convince highly
industrialized Japan and Germany that the future belongs to
Communism while the attempt continues to undermine our
ties with Western Europe.

On a day-to-day basis the Soviet leaders alternate between
smiles and frowns in their dealings with us, and the smiles are
always welcome. But the Kremlin's long-term objective remains clear. It is to isolate us politically, economically, ideo-
logically from the people and the resources of the world
beyond our shores.

This, in turn, confronts us with a haunting question that
goes far beyond what may be done to slow down the arms
race between the United States and Russia: How can we

create the essential common ground with the non-Communist two-thirds of mankind upon which both our national security and world peace depend?

Those who concern themselves with moral factors in international relationships are often charged with lack of realism. But what about the realism of their critics?

The difference lies in what we mean by power. Many 'realists' define power as a complex of military forces, industrial capacity, stores of nuclear weapons and bases from which to deliver them, radar warning systems, dispersion of cities, stockpiles, communications, geography and allies.

This definition of power is all right as far as it goes, but in our modern revolutionary world it doesn't go nearly far enough.

Since the end of the Second World War the decisive power on three continents has been provided, not by armoured divisions, bombing squadrons and steel mills, but by an explosive political combination consisting of dedicated leaders, dynamic ideas and frustrated people.

This combination has already overturned the governments of China, Indonesia, Israel, India, Indochina, Burma, Ceylon, Pakistan, Tunisia, Cuba, Syria, Iraq, Morocco, Jordan, Egypt, the Sudan, Guinea, Nigeria and Ghana.

In each forced change of government since 1948, excepting only Czechoslovakia, the weight of military and industrial power has overwhelmingly favoured the *status quo*. Yet again and again the *status quo* has been forced to bow to the revolutionary political force of people and ideas.

Sometimes the changes have come with bloodshed and brutality, as in China; in other cases with dignity and compassion, as in India, Pakistan, Ghana and Tunisia.

But whether the cause be good or evil it is safe to say that the explosive combination of ideas and people will continue to upset governments, defy armies and write history.

To reaffirm this essential and forsaken dimension of power

is the New Realism. And practical recognition of the twentieth-century validity of the American Dream within this new and broader power concept not only affects our immediate national security but is the key to our ultimate hopes for peace and brotherhood.

Perhaps the most significant fact of our times is that the revolution which shaped our own history is alive and on the march again in Asia, Africa, in the Middle East and in Latin America. It may wander into wayward paths or keep to a steadier course. It may be led by saints or by sinners.

But whether it is wayward or steady, whether dedicated men or impostors march at its head, it is carrying everything before it. And all those who would influence its course must speak its language.

At every great public conference in the three awakening continents, it is the traditional idea of freedom first written into our own Declaration of Independence which emerges as a stated, agreed-upon national objective.

In 1955, for example, at the Bandung Conference in Indonesia, representatives of twenty-eight Asian and African nations came together to seek a common perspective and objective. Virtually every form of society known to human history had its representatives on the scene.

But in defiance of these differences, and in defiance of what some of the leaders themselves may have personally felt, they signed their names to a series of resolutions which could be grouped under four heads. They were :

1. An end to colonial rule.

2. A full measure of human dignity regardless of race, creed or colour.

3. Rapid economic development, broadly shared.

4. The abolition of war and the creation of expanding areas of good will.

These concepts are no more and no less than an assertion from these decisive, restless new continents of the continuing

American Revolution for which Jefferson, Lincoln, Wilson and Franklin Roosevelt spoke so eloquently.

In today's world the greatest testimony to the political power of these ideas is that the Communists are constantly striving to steal them, to stuff them with their own distorted meanings, and to use them to destroy us.

The saddest commentary on the failure of our American leadership to grasp the significance of this development was provided by the State Department official who remarked of Bandung, 'We view it with benevolent indifference.'

This brings the challenge into clear focus. Can the new leadership elected in 1960 put our heritage, capacity, and energy to work in American foreign and domestic policy?

The challenge cannot be met with stepped-up doses of public relations and psychological warfare. It will not be enough for us to point our finger at the fraudulent slogans of the Russians, or cynically to rewrite a shopworn and insensitive diplomacy in the stirring language of Jefferson.

The peoples of Latin America, Asia, Africa and the Middle East will judge us, they will repose their trust in us or withhold it, not by our rhetoric about the Rights of Man but by what we do or fail to do to advance those rights within our own nation and in the world community.

Most emphatically the New Realism is not an invitation to pompous international moralizing. A self-conscious concentration on moral superiority can encourage the conviction that the way to deal with evil in the world is either to withdraw into an isolationist Fortress America or to sally forth to subdue evil with force.

It can blind us to the brute facts of human political existence, to the conflict of national interests, economic competition, popular emotional attitudes and national aspirations.

To these pitfalls there can be added the revulsion other peoples feel when they discover that those who affect the tone and manner of godliness are not really better than other men – and hence, if not better, must be much worse.

Self-styled 'realists' are everlastingly right when they say that peace cannot be created with words. But they are wrong when they discount the power of universal, deeply held convictions about human dignity, brotherhood, freedom and opportunity in world affairs.

A new leadership in Washington, therefore, must reassert in a new international context the political, social and economic principles which have furnished the strength and driving force of our democratic society. Our task is no more and no less than to demonstrate in practical terms that the American Revolution, as Jefferson once said, 'belongs to all mankind'.

The demands upon us are therefore twofold. Unless we proceed, in the absence of an effective disarmament agreement, to create an adequate defence barrier, there may be no free world left to save. Yet unless vital, free societies can be developed behind that barrier, and our own democracy strengthened and revitalized, the universal dream of dignity and opportunity may be destroyed without a shot being fired.

Once we begin to move in partnership with others to help create societies in which moral values are free to grow, the present negative image of America will change rapidly. We will again become what the world expects us to be : a strong, brave and generous society, opposed to any nation that pushes other people around or to any doctrine that ignores the rights of the individual, using its vast national power and moral influence to promote the ultimate good not simply for ourselves but for all men.

Our ability to play this role depends in large measure on the degree to which our generation of Americans rededicates itself to the principles of the American Dream.

As never before, domestic and foreign affairs have become one and the same thing. The old notion of two self-sealing worlds of politics, one at home and the other abroad, is gone forever. If we fail in one place, we are denied the means of success in the other.

The world which was always round has suddenly become very small as well. And in that small, round world there are four fundamental questions, that demand our immediate and dedicated attention.

The first relates to our capacity to live together in harmony and effectiveness.

The second relates to our capacity for sustained economic growth.

The third relates to the quality of our culture, of our communities, and of our living.

The fourth relates to our capacity to understand the scope and thrust of living in a twentieth-century world and to create a practical basis for common action with other people who, like us, cherish freedom and the right to develop in their own way.

I deeply believe that these four powerful elements are now merging to form a fourth political consensus which is waiting only the spark of a new national leadership. In the subsequent chapters we shall examine the evidence and consider the requirements.

PART II

The Evolution of the American Dream

There has always been the American Dream. But the very opportunities which seem to make that Dream more realizable in America than in any other land have been so great that each generation has seized them and tried to make the most of them for the favoured few.

Every now and then the Dream therefore has seemed to fade. But always a reaction has come and the people have risen again to make the Dream come true.

JAMES TRUSLOW ADAMS

CHAPTER IV

The Assurance of Political Liberty

BEFORE proceeding to a discussion of the three-dimensional challenge which we face it may be well to review briefly the nature of the American Dream and its roots in history.

Such a review will necessarily cover familiar ground. Yet in the retelling we may come to see that this challenge is no more and no less than the expression within a new global framework of old conflicts and objectives, which previous generations of Americans have been called upon to meet and master on narrower ground.

Our experience as an independent nation began with a statement that political liberty is the prerequisite and framework alike for all other freedoms and liberties – religious, social, economic and cultural.

Moreover, from the very outset we related political liberty directly to a soaring but explicit new vision of man.

'We hold these truths to be self-evident,' the Declaration of Independence reads, 'that all men are created equal, that they are endowed by their Creator with certain inalienable rights, that among these are life, liberty, and the pursuit of happiness. That to secure these rights, governments are instituted among men, deriving their just powers from the consent of the governed.'

Where could there be a sharper contrast with the current Communist notion that the individual has no social and political rights except those that the state deems proper to confer on him?

Our Declaration affirms that there are elements of the human personality that are inviolate and stand above the secular power of any government – and that governments justify their existence only as they protect and enrich each citizen's inalienable dignity as a human being.

35

This was a profoundly radical notion when it was first voiced – more radical, even, than the idea of Magna Carta, a charter of liberty granted by power.

We Americans deliberately proclaimed that charters of power are valid only if they are granted by free citizens. That such a notion should have been voiced by a handful of men living in a wilderness outpost of civilization who presumed to speak for all mankind, must surely have seemed a supreme act of impudence two centuries ago.

Indeed, some of the men who affixed their names to the Declaration of Independence were inclined to look upon it as a shrewd piece of wartime propaganda, which was not to be taken too seriously once independence was won from Great Britain.

When they came into control of the new federal government established in 1789, it was not surprising to see them narrow the phrase 'all men' to mean 'some men' – the few who enjoyed the special privileges of wealth, family connections and education.

These alone were to have their 'inalienable rights' pre-eminently respected and served by the new government, the control of which would be a virtual monopoly of persons like themselves.

Their insistence on this point of view made it plain that while the American War against the British had been won in 1783, the American Revolution was still in doubt. And as this became understood, more and more Americans rallied to Thomas Jefferson with his doctrine that not only must the American government be democratic in its political form, but that its practices must reflect the will of the people.

This, in essence, was the heart of the revolution which began after Jefferson's 1800 Presidential victory, and which brought into power the first national consensus of the three we considered in a previous chapter.

Jefferson viewed the principles of the Declaration of Independence not merely as an object of lip service and ritual, but as a mode of conduct. Indeed, it was for this reason that so many Federalists who were perfectly sane in other matters seemed to run amok in their violent antipathy to Jefferson.

Unless the popular movement which Jefferson headed could be checked, some asserted, the mob scenes of revolutionary France would be duplicated in America.

One of these Federalists, Fisher Ames, even pictured in his mind's eye 'the dismal glare of their burnings and scent of the loathsome steam of human victims offered in sacrifice'.

After Jefferson's election in 1801, an ancestor of mine, Timothy Dwight, President of Yale University and an ardent Federalist, believed that henceforth the nation would be 'governed by blockheads and knaves'. As a consequence, he added, 'the ties of marriage will be severed; our wives and daughters thrown into the stews; our children cast into the world from the breast and forgotten; and filial piety extinguished'.

Jefferson not only survived such nonsense but proceeded to expand his new political concepts of human dignity to the entire world. In 1801 he expressed the hope that the establishment in America of a deeply rooted democratic government would be 'a standing monument, an example for the aim and imitation of the people of other countries'.

It would show the world, he said, 'that a free government is also the most energetic; that the inquiry which has been excited among the mass of mankind by our revolution and its consequences, will ameliorate the condition of man over a great portion of the globe'.

Here, transcending the language of the Declaration of Independence but evolving directly and logically from it, was a new restatement of our national purpose.

So it was with Jefferson in the subsequent acts of his Administration. Whenever the opportunity arose, he continued to restate our national purpose so that Americans everywhere would understand why they were doing what they were doing.

In 1803, for example, when Jefferson consummated the historic Louisiana Purchase, a lesser man in his place might have allowed the act to stand in the public mind as a welcome assurance that our navigation rights on the Mississippi River would be secure.

But not Jefferson. He assigned a meaning to the acquisition of the Louisiana Territory that made it fit into a great design for the extension and perpetuation of free societies.

'America itself,' he said, was 'an empire for liberty,' and Louisiana, in its own way, would extend the scope of freedom and reinforce its foundations.

'The addition to the great republican family of this hemisphere of a country so extensive, so fertile as Louisiana,' he wrote, 'has secured the blessings of civil and religious freedom to millions yet unborn.

'By enlarging the empire of liberty, we provide new sources of renovation, should its principle, at any time, degenerate in those portions of our country which gave them birth.'

Indeed, this soaring vision of an empire of liberty led the heirs of Jefferson to conceive of America as a New Eden, where man himself could be reborn as a New Adam. The world and history lay all before him.

Untouched and undefiled by the heritage of hatred and corruption carried over from the past, the American would be the individual standing alone, self-reliant and self-propelling, ready to confront whatever awaited him with the aid of his own unique and inherent resources.

'Our national birth,' said the *Democratic Review* in 1839, 'was the beginning of a new history . . . which separates us from the past and connects us with the future.'

Built into the heart of Jefferson's view of our national purpose was his own unqualified allegiance to the Party of Hope. He was determined to leave a political legacy guaranteeing that his successors in the Democratic party would perpetuate the same allegiance.

The Whig adversaries against whom they contended, and over whom they won another historic victory under the leadership of Andrew Jackson, remained the adherents of the Party of Memory.

At best, the Party of Memory clung to the view that the safest policy for America was to stand still. At worst, it expressed a reactionary nostalgia for the days when things were thought to be better for the 'rich and well-born' before the Jeffersonian concept of a New Eden took hold.

But in the 1850's, as we have seen, the geographic, economic and cultural elements of the growing storm over slavery, rendered the Democratic party as it was then constituted increasingly obsolete.

Forces that were apathetic or hostile to the inalienable dignity of the individual helped destroy the Jeffersonian heritage and crippled the party as an instrument of national leadership for two successive generations.

The new Republican party under Lincoln, in a sense stronger at birth than it has ever been in maturity, moved to the forefront to defend both freedom and union. It thus became a temporary but genuine champion of the Party of Hope.

After the Civil War, the times required us to move beyond the Jeffersonian, Jacksonian and Lincolnian concepts of liberty to open up still newer frontiers lying in the direction of social and economic liberty. But first came the long and tumultuous process of digesting the human strains that were to be both the objects and the authors of new conceptions of the American Dream.

CHAPTER V

A Nation of Immigrants

No OTHER people has ever attempted the American project of building a united nation out of so many diverse human strains.

A single statistic suggests the magnitude of the undertaking. Between 1820 and 1920 seven out of every ten of the 62 million people who uprooted themselves from their native soil to seek a better life in other lands came to the United States.

In doing this, they continued a process that had been under way for a century before the American Revolution. On the eve of the Revolution, the people of England's thirteen colonies included such widely diverse elements that the recently arrived Tom Paine could say in *Common Sense,* 'Europe, not England, is the parent country of America.'

Of the fifty-six signers of the Declaration of Independence, eighteen were of non-English descent. Eight of them were first-generation immigrants.

Who were these early Americans, and what brought them to these shores?

The modern philosopher-poet, George Santayana, himself an immigrant, reflected on the question and answered, 'The fortunate, the deeply rooted, and the lazy remained at home. The wilder instincts or dissatisfactions of others tempted them beyond the horizon. The American is accordingly the most adventurous, or the descendant of the most adventurous of Europeans.'

Two groups of newcomers to America were exceptions to this selection by free choice.

The first were the Negro slaves from Africa who, at the time of the Revolution, constituted one-fifth of our total population. The others were the English convicts who were sent here to serve out their terms at forced labour. In 1776 they numbered some fifty thousand.

With the exception of these two contingents, the great body of the early settlers were overwhelmingly alike in two respects.

Whether they came here for religious, economic or political motives or a combination of the three, they were men and women who had deliberately rejected the past. They were volunteers for membership in the Party of Hope, consciously determined to live for the future.

They were also poor. Indeed, nearly half of them came to America under an arrangement where the ship captain on arrival sold their services to an employer for a term of two to seven years to pay for their passage.

The common experience of acute hardships, alleviated by the miracle of America itself, was thus shared by many millions of Americans.

This formative experience accounts for some of the most appealing aspects of the American character. It helps explain our willingness to aid other people who are in want, our persistent good will, our lack of class consciousness, our spirit of trust in others, our tolerance of differences, our optimism about the future.

But there was also a darker side to the immigration process. The clash between successive waves of new settlers and those who had arrived earlier often expressed itself in ugly forms. Indeed, much of American political and social history was shaped by a cycle of conflicts and adjustments as successive waves of newcomers struggled to find a secure place in American society.

These tensions date to the colonial era, when the older Anglo-Saxon colonial stock began to view with alarm the arrival here of each new batch of non-English immigrants.

The arguments they advanced for restricting newcomers have a familiar ring even in our own time.

They charged that the new immigrants were politically

'backward'; that they were the agents of a mysterious but dangerous religious conspiracy; that they were paupers who would soon become public charges; or that they were criminals who posed a constant threat to life and property.

The most effective answer to these accusations came from the new immigrants themselves, who filled out the companies, battalions and regiments of George Washington's patriot armies that won America's independence from England.

A few years later when it came time to write a new charter of government, the Constitutional Convention rejected all proposals to cut off further immigration. Instead, provisions were made to assure the country a continuing cosmopolitan character. The spirit of tolerance and accommodation which they expressed had no equal anywhere in the world of that day.

The Constitution itself forbade the Congress to bar the immigration or importation of aliens prior to 1808. It forbade any religious test for public office.

Moreover, it provided that any foreigner of a designated age who had been a citizen for seven years was eligible for election to the House of Representatives and, after an added two years of citizenship, to the Senate. If they were citizens when the Constitution went into effect, they could also aspire to the Presidency, though thereafter the incumbent had to be a 'natural born citizen'.

Finally, the Constitution empowered the Congress to establish a uniform method of naturalization. The first Congress fixed two years as the period of naturalization.

'Whether subjects of Kings or citizens of free states,' declared one member, 'they will find it in their interest to be good citizens, and neither their religious nor political opinion can injure us, if we have good laws, well executed.'

History was to speak a tremendous amen to this prophecy. Yet it was not spoken without stubborn resistance. Within six years after the Constitution was adopted, the 'well-bred and the well-born', in a renewal of their hostility to the strangers in their midst, launched a vigorous counter-attack.

In 1795, the Federalist party, temporarily dominant in the new government, lengthened the naturalization period for new immigrants from two to five years. Its object was to curb the rising power of Jefferson's party, which had attracted the majority of the newly arrived immigrants.

When it developed that the Jeffersonians could not be curbed so easily, the Federalists resorted to passing the more drastic Alien and Sedition Laws.

The Alien part of those laws increased the naturalization period from five to fourteen years. During this period the President was empowered to deport any alien he judged to be 'dangerous to the peace and safety of the United States'.

The chief targets were the Scotch-Irish, described by one New England Federalist as 'the most God-provoking Democrats on this side of Hell'. A second major target were the ardently pro-Jefferson Germans, under the leadership of Peter and Frederick Muhlenberg in Pennsylvania.

The Sedition parts of the Federalist laws were designed to suppress the scores of outspoken pro-Jefferson editors and pamphleteers of French, British and Irish nativity who had become American citizens. They could be fined and imprisoned for 'seditious utterances or writings' against the President or Congress – however innocent the remarks might appear to non-Federalist minds.

After the Federalists were overthrown in the sweeping Jefferson victory of 1800, the newly elected majority in Congress promptly repealed the Alien and Sedition Laws and cut the time span for citizenship from fourteen to five years, where it remains to this day.

The Old Guard Federalist hostility to European newcomers, however, continued to simmer beneath the surface of American politics. It erupted in 1814 at the Federalists' Convention in Hartford with the demand that the Constitution be amended to exclude all naturalized citizens from federal office.

Had this proposal been in effect previously it would have prevented Alexander Hamilton from serving Washington as

Secretary of the Treasury, and Albert Gallatin from serving Jefferson in the same capacity.

The Federalist proposal was suddenly discredited by the dramatic news of the New Orleans victory of Andrew Jackson, himself a first-generation American of Scotch-Irish origin.

Yet the human struggle was to be a continuing one. No sooner had one generation achieved a balance between the declining interests of the firmly rooted older stock and the most recent wave of newcomers, than a fresh influx of immigrants from Europe upset the balance and set off a new series of conflicts.

From the ratification of the Constitution to the close of the War of 1812, the immigrant flow from Europe was about 250,000 in all. A generation later the wave of immigrants seemed to be expanding geometrically : half a million in the 1830's; over a million and a half in the 1840's; and two and one-half million in the 1850's.

Although most of the immigrants continued to come from Northern Europe, the proportion of Germans and particularly South Irish sharply increased. This led to new economic and political tensions in the whole of America's social order.

Bad crops, worse landlords, and the failure of the 1848 Revolution persuaded a million and a half Germans to move to America in the period of 1830–1860. Most of them settled around the Great Lakes and throughout the Midwest.

During the Civil War these newly arrived Germans were recruited in such numbers for the Union armies that in whole divisions all military orders were issued in German.

The South Irish came in even greater numbers between 1830 and 1860. The total was nearly two million, half of whom arrived after the potato famine of 1846.

They were largely of peasant stock. But because they were insecure in their strange new surroundings, most of them chose to seek work under appalling conditions in the jam-packed cities. There, at least, they could be near their relatives and priests.

In their congested urban surroundings, the Irish had one solid advantage over most of their immigrant neighbours. They spoke English. And since male white suffrage was by this time universal, the American democratic political system provided a ladder they could climb to positions of influence denied them by other means.

Inevitably they became the political spokesmen for other recently arrived immigrants who shared their hard lot, but who lacked a knowledge of English with which to protest.

Descendants of earlier immigrant waves continued bitterly to oppose the Irish newcomers. Employers were urged to post signs over factory gates reading 'NO IRISH NEED APPLY'. Members of Congress supported legislation 'to protect our natural born workers from this competition of foreign mechanics and labourers'.

As the old American Protestant stock saw Catholic churches, convents and parochial schools rise in their midst, they gave increasing attention to the demagogues who warned that 'Rome is plotting to capture the American government'.

Opposition gangs sprouted in many cities under such flamboyant titles as Black Snakes, Tigers, Rough Skins, Red Necks, Thunderbolts, Gladiators, Screw Boats, Stay Lates, Hard Times, Plug-Uglies, Dips, and Blood Tubs, many of which ultimately joined together in a militant secret society called the Order of the Star-Spangled Banner.

Since its members refused to answer questions about their organization or its objectives, Horace Greeley called them the Know-Nothing party.

In the elections of 1854 the Know-Nothings, now officially labelled the American party, demanded exclusion of all foreign-born and all Catholics from public office and twenty-one years' residence in America before voting. Its vote was so large that many observers believed that it would soon replace the Whigs as the major opposition party to the Democrats.

But again the deeply rooted democratic reaction against intolerance and extremism which is so stubbornly characteristic of American society reasserted itself. When the Know-Nothings pushed through a series of pro-slavery resolutions at their 1855 convention they were doomed as a national party.

As we have seen, the new liberal anti-slavery consensus expressed itself through the new Republican party, which was wise enough to woo the new immigrants vigorously.

Carl Schurz, an 1848 German immigrant, persuaded the 1860 Republican Convention to declare itself in opposition to any stiffening of naturalization requirements or the abridging in any way of the rights of foreign-born citizens. As an extra inducement to the immigrant voter, the platform pledged the newcomers free homesteads in the public domain.

During the tragic conflict that began in 1861 the valour and dedication of the Irish and German regiments in the Union armies sharply reduced the agitation against all immigrants.

But the melting-pot had barely begun its work. Between the end of the Civil War and 1917, some 27 million more people migrated to the United States. This exceeded the entire population of 1850.

This influx was encouraged by massive subsidies of free federal lands in the West which led to a tremendous railroad-building boom in the three decades following the Civil War.

To help create freight and passenger traffic, agents of the American railroads moved throughout Western Europe recruiting immigrant settlers who could be established on homesteads along the rights of way. The transformation of the Central Northwest into a New Scandinavia, with its concentrations of Norwegians, Swedes and Danes, owes much to this process.

But beginning in the 1880's the security of the older immigrant elements once more began to be challenged by a new tidal wave of immigrants. This time it consisted of Italians, Poles, Czechs, Lithuanians, Jews, Russians, Slovaks, Hungarians, Serbs, Croats and Greeks from Southern and Eastern Europe.

Many of these newcomers left their homes for the same

familiar reasons : inability to make a living as tenant farmers on vast feudal estates, political and religious persecution, oppressive systems of military servitude, or simply the hoped-for opportunity to make fortunes in America.

An increasing number, however, were actively recruited by representatives of the fast-growing new industries of New England, New York, Pennsylvania and New Jersey, and the Western mining areas on which these industries depended for coal, copper, iron and other raw materials.

Mine and factory owners were only too glad to prepay the steamship passage of immigrants who were eager to learn the new industrial techniques and willing to work for low wages.

With their arrival in increasing numbers, we saw a repetition of the same familiar cycle of cultural shock, alienation, reconciliation and gradual assimilation that had marked the clashing of immigrant groups in our earlier days.

In 1892 our official census-taker declared that there was no longer any Western frontier. Increasingly the ships arriving almost daily from Europe began to add their masses of newcomers to the already overcrowded city slums.

The desperate scramble for available jobs on any terms made effective labour organization difficult. Private social work groups, health agencies and public playgrounds expanded rapidly. But they touched no more than a small corner of the human problems created by this newest immigration influx.

In the gulf between generations, parental authority in immigrant families was weakened. In the ugly setting of the slums, family life was undercut at every turn.

Unable to speak English, often illiterate, clinging for security to the old ways, the parents of these families began to see their American-educated children looking down on them as 'foreigners'.

Inevitably juvenile delinquency among the children of the new immigrants became widespread. At first the street gangs served as vigilante forces that protected various immigrant enclaves from the ethnic or religious-inspired attacks of their neighbours. Later some of the vigilantes diverted their energies into crime in order to gain the material status that seemed beyond their reach through legal means.

During the remaining years of the century, influential groups displayed mounting concern over the changes they believed the rising flood of immigrants would force on American society.

Organized labour, in order to protect its hard-won gains, began to advocate cutting down the flood of new workers from South and East Europe who were prepared to work at any wage.

Although businessmen had a corresponding economic interest in encouraging the immigrant influx they began to worry about the social and political disturbances that might be sparked by radical foreigners.

Political leaders of Anglo-Saxon origin once more warned that the Nordic race 'of soldiers, sailors, adventurers, explorers, rulers, organizers, and aristocrats', who were said to have 'created America', would soon be engulfed and its blood corrupted by the immigrant tide of 'peasants from the Alpine race'.

The advocates of immigration restriction not only by number but by national origin as well soon hit upon the literacy test. Three times such tests as a basis of admission to the United States were enacted into legislation by Congress. And three times this legislation was vetoed by broader-visioned Presidents.

The third President to do so was Woodrow Wilson. In his veto message of 1915, he observed that the legislation embodied a test not of personal fitness but of opportunity; that it was wrong for the Congress to refuse admittance to those immigrants who lacked 'one of the chief of the opportunities they seek here, the opportunity of education'.

Mr Wilson's first veto was sustained. Two years later, however, in the confused atmosphere generated by our plunge into the European war, another literacy test bill was pushed through the Congress. This time, over Wilson's second veto, it became law.

The final step in the restriction of immigration was taken in the 'twenties. The goad was fear that a deluge from war-stricken Europe would 'take bread from the mouths of native workers' and, as businessmen believed, 'propagate radical and subversive ideas' that had been learned in the school of the Russian Revolution.

A contributory cause, sometimes forgotten, was the abrupt collapse of the American economy in 1920. The recession of that year struck agriculture in the Middle West and the South with particular severity.

This led to the resurgence of Know-Nothingism under a different but familiar name. The Ku Klux Klan, rooted in the small towns and rural areas, deliberately incited hatred against Catholics, Jews, Negroes and the foreign-born, and lashed out against the fast-growing political power of the cities. By 1925 it claimed a membership of 4 million.

In 1921 and 1924, Congress passed legislation to limit all immigration, but most particularly immigration from Southern and Eastern Europe.

Through restrictions whose concepts still remain on the statute books, each nationality was granted an annual quota of immigrants, based on the existing percentage of citizens from each nationality group in the total population. The obvious effect was to discriminate against the Slavs and Mediterranean peoples and to favour immigration from Northern Europe.

Changing times and the filling up of the American continent had modified the Statue of Liberty's call for Europe's 'huddled masses yearning to breathe free'. But no one can dispute the extraordinary democratic achievement of the American melting-pot. Nothing comparable has been attempted in the long history of the human race.

Each nationality group has made its own contribution to the enrichment of our nation, to our arts and sciences, to our strength in time of war. Imperceptibly each has been merged into the composite American.

In 1924 the conflicts between old and new Americans were still strong enough to deny Al Smith, a Catholic, the Democratic nomination for the Presidency. Four years later, however, he was nominated and received almost as many votes in defeat as Calvin Coolidge had received in victory.

Though he lost several states in the Democratic South, more significant for future developments was the fact that Al Smith broke the Republican control over many Northern cities.

Thirty-two years later we face the possibility of another historic advance. In 1960 a Catholic may not only be nominated for the Presidency or the Vice-Presidency; he may in fact be elected.

In the choice of mayors, governors, and senators all signs of the struggle between the old and the new immigrants have virtually disappeared. On this plane of politics the Party of Hope appears to have won a dramatic victory over the Party of Memory.

Thus, within recent years, a Pole was elected Governor and then Senator from Maine. A Jew was elected Governor of Connecticut and re-elected with the greatest majority in the state's history. An Italian was elected and re-elected Governor of Massachusetts.

A Catholic Irishman was elected United States Senator from Lutheran Minnesota. A Czech was elected and re-elected Governor of Ohio and then elected to the United States Senate. His successor as Governor is an Italian.

An Indian from the distant Punjab, now a citizen of California, was elected to Congress. He has now been joined there by a Japanese from Hawaii.

In such ways we have demonstrated the profoundly democratic, all-inclusive base of our American political system. We have proved that the eagerness of the immigrant to cast his lot with America is matched by America's willingness to have him do so.

We have shown that our national instincts for justice can successfully cope with racial and religious extremism.

In 1944 Archbishop Francis J. Spellman suggested the reasons : 'All fair-minded Americans oppose bigotry,' he said, 'not only from a sense of justice but also from a sense of safety. For, if tolerated, it can be directed at any race or religion and then may rebound against all of them.'

How long will it take us to learn that this truth also applies to the relationship between American whites and American Negroes?

CHAPTER VI

The Democracy of Knowledge

THERE was room here in America for successive waves of immigrants and the material means to sustain them. There was also a political system which placed no legal bars, as in other countries, on where the immigrant could settle and what he could do.

Still, a nation is not welded together by physical space, by natural resources, or by the mobility of its inhabitants. Something more is needed to instill in the hearts and minds of different human beings a common devotion to the institutions of liberty.

The situation called for a special adjunct to the national melting-pot and the American public school system provided it.

We were the first nation in history to provide the mass of our people with an education hitherto limited almost everywhere to the privileged few.

We were first to fashion an educational system into a social force that levelled class differences.

We were first to place all our young people on an equal footing as they began the contests of life.

We were first to bring together in our classrooms children of every ethnic origin and to undertake systematically to implant in their consciousness the ways and means of living together in mutual respect.

Indeed, the extraordinary effectiveness of our public school system in easing the difference between potentially antagonistic groups helps explain why the present-day fight to accord the Negro first-class citizenship finds its focal point in the fight to integrate our public schools.

Those who would deny the Negro the equality of opportunity that is rightfully his would not now be fighting to keep the public schools segregated if those schools had failed as instruments of democracy.

In a topsy-turvy way these last-ditch opponents of school integration pay the American school system its highest tribute as a democratizing instrument when they say they would rather see their schools closed than integrated.

As in so many other matters, the tradition of democratic education in America began with Thomas Jefferson, who placed universal education in a direct relationship with the principles of human freedom and equality that he set forth in the Declaration of Independence.

'Liberty and learning,' he said, 'each must lean on the other for their mutual and surest support.'

If liberty is denied, learning withers or is crowded into narrow channels. Conversely, if learning suffers that kind of fate, then liberty is denied the means by which to defend or to enlarge itself.

Therefore, Jefferson gave to universal education a central place in the social and political structure of the democracy he helped build. Nor did he wait for the Revolution to be won to translate his ideas into action.

As Governor of Virginia in 1779, he sent a measure to the

Virginia Assembly entitled, 'A Bill for the More General Diffusion of Knowledge'.

He summoned all his strength and eloquence to champion the right of all to have access to elementary education, and the right of the most talented youth from every economic class to the higher education they merited.

The ideas of democratic education, to which Jefferson first gave currency, were seized upon and developed by successive generations of Americans. The new influx of immigrants provided a steady impetus toward universal public education.

Few pleas were more eloquent or influential than that made in 1830 by the Working Men's Committee in Philadelphia. This remarkable group realized that the basic interests of American workers extended far beyond improved wages, shorter hours, and better working conditions.

Like Jefferson, they understood the close ties between education, equality of opportunity and self-government. In their report on the state of public instruction in Pennsylvania, they had this to say :

> The original element of despotism is a monopoly of talent, which consigns the multitude to comparative ignorance and secures the balance of knowledge on the side of the rich and the rulers.
>
> When the Committee contemplate their own condition and that of the great mass of their fellow-labourers, when they look around on the glaring inequality of society, they are constrained to believe that until the means of equal instruction shall be equally secured to all, liberty is but an unmeaning word and equality but an empty shadow, whose substance to be realized must first be planted by an equal education and proper training in the minds, in the habits, in the manners and in the feelings of the community.

The same arguments were advanced and refined by Horace Mann, who gave up a lucrative law practice in the 1830's to become the principal leader of a movement to strengthen the public schools of Massachusetts. The impact of his successful efforts there encouraged similar advances throughout the country.

Horace Mann observed that the glitter of most contemporary European kingdoms arose amid 'millions of paupers who cower and shiver at its base'.

In the fullness of time, he warned, their privations combined with their ignorance would threaten the shining superstructure of the privileged social order built on top of them.

Mann also saw that his native Massachusetts, by its advanced industrial condition and the scope of its commercial enterprises, lay more exposed than any other state in the Union to the clash of 'fatal extremes of overgrown wealth and desperate poverty'.

How could a social explosion be avoided? The answer was universal education.

Education, he said, 'gives each man the independence and the means by which he can resist the selfishness of other men'. It does more than 'disarm the poor of their hostility toward the rich. It prevents them being poor', and thus removes the pretexts on which the poor would avenge themselves against the rich.

In referring to a republic without adequate education he added :

Such a republic may grow in numbers and in wealth. Its armies may be invincible, and its fleets may strike terror into nations on the opposite sides of the globe at the same hour.

But if such a republic be devoid of intelligence, it will only the more closely resemble an obscene giant who has waxed strong in his youth and grown wanton in his strength; whose brain has been developed only in the region of the appetites and passions and not in the organs of reason and conscience; and who, therefore, is boastful of his bulk alone and glories in the weight of his heel and in the destruction of his arm.

Such a republic, with all its noble capacities for benefi-
cence, will rush with the speed of a whirlwind to an
ignominious end. And all good men of aftertime would be
fain to weep over its downfall, did not their scorn and
contempt at its folly and its wickedness repress all sorrow
for its fate.

In such expressions from widely different sources – from
Thomas Jefferson, a committee of Philadelphia working-men,
and a Massachusetts lawyer – we find the crusading spirit of
the Party of Hope, buoying up the democratic purpose which
created the American public school.

In our century the brilliance and dedication of countless
other educational pioneers have carried the tradition forward.

Many authorities, to be sure, believe that our modern public
school system has to some extent sacrificed quality for quantity. Yet whatever the sacrifice, it was made under pressure of
our commitment to educate the great mass of our people
instead of a select few.

It was made under the obligation to provide millions of
children from diverse ethnic backgrounds with a common set
of shared schoolroom experiences and thus to lay the basis for
the community life they would later share as citizens.

It was made under the necessity to provide a social anchor
which could offer stability to millions of uprooted families,
and in many cases, to serve as a substitute parent for young
Americans who had almost no point of effective contact with
their immigrant mothers and fathers.

The unprecedented challenge of the American melting-pot
burdened the public schools with social and political tasks of
prime importance. If there was too small a reserve of time and
energy left in some cases to further the cultivation of excellence, it is understandable.

Our complex system of private and state-supported colleges
and universities now provides a higher education each year to
nearly three million young Americans. It is interesting to note

that the only other nation which has contemplated an educational system of such magnitude is the Soviet Union.

Space permits only this brief outline of the extraordinary democratizing influence of our system of public education. Yet one final comment seems appropriate.

Our public school system will never be finished with its work of training children of diverse backgrounds for citizenship in a democracy. In future years, however, we will be in a better position to review and strengthen our *standards* of training and the complex chain of influences which play a part in their formulation.

These include the admissions systems of our state-supported colleges and universities; the conditions on which students should remain in these institutions; the connection between these institutions and their departments of education, between the latter and the teachers' colleges, and between the teachers' colleges and the local schools, their boards of education and their tax resources.

Our object must be to cultivate young American minds to the maximum degree of excellence that each can absorb regardless of family income. The need to do this is made all the more imperative by the enormous opportunities and requirements of the world which our young people are now entering.

Household knowledge and conventional wisdom are no longer a sufficient basis for self-government in a world where the problems of survival are intermeshed with infinitely complex scientific and technological questions. These questions form a special and continuing challenge to our whole theory of education for freedom.

Our educational system, therefore, bears a growing burden to validate our basic democratic assumption that the electorate will know enough and be wise enough to pass a thoughtful judgment on the crucially important decisions made by its elected and appointed officials.

CHAPTER VII

The Expansion of Economic Liberty

IN THIS compressed historical review, we have already spoken of three things : the evolution of our concepts of political liberty, of social equality in a nation formed of immigrants, and of public education that was both the father and the child of the preceding two.

Next we must set in place the evolution of our concept of economic liberty that moved abreast of these other evolutionary lines.

From the birth of the federal government until 1861, the heirs of Thomas Jefferson and Alexander Hamilton argued the question of whether the future of America lay in agriculture or in commerce and industry.

But on one principle, both were agreed : the individual, by the use of his own wits and will, was to organize production and distribution. And this the typical American was ready and eager to do.

In the 1830's de Tocqueville wrote : 'It is strange to see with what feverish ardour the Americans pursue their own welfare and to watch the vague dread that constantly torments them lest they should not have chosen the shortest path which may lead to it.'

This restlessness was and is the source of an experimental approach to economic life, of a will to evade the bondage of class opinions and prejudices, to strike through the form to the substance of existing facts, to seek better economic results by direct pragmatic action.

Mrs Frances Trollope, who came here from England a few years before de Tocqueville arrived from France, wrote of an unnamed man, who was an embodiment of this spirit :

> When I first became his neighbour, himself, his wife and four children, were living in one room. . . . He made an

engagement with the proprietor of a wooded hill by which all the wood he could fell was to be his own.

His unwearied industry made this a profitable bargain, and from the proceeds he purchased the materials for building a comfortable frame house; he did the work almost entirely himself. He then got a job for cutting rails, and as he could cut twice as many in a day as any other man in the neighbourhood, he made a good thing of it.

He then let half his pretty house, which was admirably constructed, with an ample portico, that kept it always cool. His next step was contracting for building a wooden bridge, and when I left Mohawk he had fitted his half of the building as an hotel and grocery store; and I have no doubt that every sun that sets sees him a richer man than when it rose.

He hopes to make his son a lawyer, and I have little doubt that he will live to see him sit in Congress. When this time arrives, the wood-cutter's son will rank with any other member of Congress, not of courtesy, but of right, and the idea that his origin is a disadvantage, will never occur to the imagination of the most exalted of his fellow-citizens.

To this tradition of human mobility, to this faith in the power of the existing social order to work for justice, and to this restless energy allied to a belief in individual progress – to all this, one more and decisive element should be added in the list of factors which explain our rapid economic growth :

Americans never for very long allowed economics to become a self-contained subject, divorced from the directing force of ethical and political considerations.

The latter considerations, it is true, were often used in reverse to justify economic pilfering on a grand scale. Yet in our darkest hours of depression and insecurity, one demand constantly reasserted itself as a rule of action : the economic process must justify itself, not alone in terms of the physical volume of goods and services it produced, but in the clear light of two questions :

First, were the material necessities of life being produced in ways that best served the happiness of the individual?

Second, were they being produced in ways that best served the cause of a good society, governing itself along democratic lines?

The power of these two questions, and the answers they elicited, head the list of factors that enabled us to disprove the dire Marxist prophecies about the future of our capitalist society.

Despite their emphasis on individualism, Jeffersonians and Hamiltonians agreed that our basic economic objective was the welfare of the nation as a whole. The very title of the work from which they drew the economic doctrine to which they jointly subscribed – Adam Smith's *Wealth of Nations* – established this overriding national interest as the standard by which all economic activity was to be judged.

Although the work of organizing production and distribution was meant to remain in private hands, an active role in the formulation of economic policy necessarily belonged to the government. Its responsibility was to maintain conditions that would directly and indirectly assist the private enterprise system in the performance of its tasks.

On this point, our American tradition is also clear.

The Constitutional Convention in 1787 grew out of a 'rivers and harbours' convention called earlier at Annapolis, to consider ways in which trade between Virginia, Delaware, New York, New Jersey and Pennsylvania could best be fostered and regulated in their mutual interest.

Later, the Constitution itself picked up the subject and enlarged upon it in ways quite contrary to textbook notions of *laissez faire*.

For example, it was promptly agreed that federal taxation was essential for sound credit. Foreign and interstate commerce was to be regulated, so that commercial prosperity might be assured. Authors and inventors were given government guarantees on the exclusive rights to their products.

Alexander Hamilton lost little time in winning acceptance for the new government from 'the commercial and industrial interest' by a series of direct and indirect paternalistic measures.

His funding of the national debt as well as state debts with six per cent federal securities gratified holders of depreciated Revolutionary War securities. The Bank of the United States, chartered by Congress, created a sound paper currency.

Manufacturers were subsidized by a mild protective tariff, which grew less mild as the years wore on. The depressed condition of the New England fisheries was relieved by a bounty on every pound of dried codfish, payable out of the national treasury.

American ship owners, crowded out of their own harbours by competing foreign vessels, were not only granted a monopoly of the coastwise trade, but were restored to prosperity with extra benefits from the government. Only ships built in the United States and belonging to American citizens could register under the American flag. Goods on American vessels had to pay only one-fifth the custom duty paid by foreign vessels.

In succeeding years, a seemingly endless number of government subsidies were granted to many different interests.

In 1808, for instance, Albert Gallatin, Jefferson's Secretary of the Treasury, complained of the slowness with which internal improvements were being undertaken. He attributed this to the scarcity of private capital.

Gallatin therefore urged the federal government to finance the construction of roads and canals, and then sell them to private corporations, which presumably would be free to charge whatever the traffic would bear.

Between 1810 and 1866, with this object in view, the federal government granted private individuals and corporations nearly seven million acres of public land (an area larger than the State of Massachusetts) to subsidize canal-building alone. This was in addition to the direct contribution of federal funds to such projects, along with the direct federal subscription of the stock in the privately owned companies.

In 1845, the pattern of shipping subsidies established in 1789 was broadened to include the United States mail as well as the use of the Navy and State Department to promote the sale of manufactured goods in the Far East. The subsidies then, as now, took the form of direct payment by the postal department to specific shipping lines over and beyond the actual cost of carrying the mail.

The railroads were the biggest beneficiaries of all. A staggering total of 183 million acres of public-owned land was given to the railroads by the federal government without charge. This area was almost as large as the thirteen original states, and considerably larger than Texas.

These holdings, which included not only timber reserves but valuable mining rights, were later sold by the railroads to private persons for huge profits.

Nor was this all. Over the years American railroads have received more than a billion dollars in direct federal subsidies to promote new construction. This is in addition to loans made since 1932 by the Reconstruction Finance Corporation and by the Federal Emergency Administration on terms far more generous than any private bank could provide.

Other direct aids to the railroads included the lowering of the import duty on railroad iron, mail service contracts over and beyond the postage income, and the free grant of rights of way over public land.

Since our earliest days American agriculture has also benefited from subsidies which total tens of billions of dollars.

Between 1785 and 1789, several private corporations were allowed to purchase public lands at prices as low as five cents an acre for resale to settlers at a far higher figure. Several of these sales were for areas larger that the State of Rhode Island.

The most impressive and perhaps most creative action of all was the Homestead Act, which Congress passed in 1862. By its terms 160 acres of public land were granted free to each family head who would agree to cultivate them, provided only that he had 'never borne arms against the United States government'.

The free grants under this law amounted in the aggregate to an area seven times the size of the State of Pennsylvania.

The government's contribution to the expansion of our economy took on a broader meaning after the Civil War, when concepts of economic liberty, once suited to an agrarian society, had to be redefined for a society that was rapidly becoming industrialized.

As the nineteenth century drew to a close, the organization of production and distribution had gradually ceased to be an individual family project tied largely to local markets. It was becoming a combination of many hands brought together in corporations, serving a national and international market through complicated communication channels.

It followed that the well-being of each individual no longer depended primarily on the wisdom and courage he showed as an individual producer and consumer, as was the case when free frontier lands were available for anybody who had the enterprise to settle on them.

The agricultural frontier was being overshadowed by the new frontier of the great industrial cities with their enormously costly concentrations of machines.

In that new frontier, the social order seemed to be dividing into a small handful of supercapitalists on the one side, and on the other, an increasing mass of men and women who owned nothing except the strength of their hands, backs and minds.

In the face of this sober new challenge, American politics slowly but steadily came to its own rescue. As it grew clear that the well-being of the individual had come to depend in great measure on the interaction of impersonal forces over which society in general had no control, we evolved and gave meaning to a new concept of the 'public interest'.

Shaped by such books as Henry George's *Progress and Poverty* and Herbert Croly's *Promise of American Life,* it gradually came to prevail over the theories of the economic Darwinians with their biological notions about 'the survival of the fittest'.

The new concept of 'the public interest' asserted that apart from any rights of ownership and management, the government had a right and duty to break up monopolistic concentrations of economic power that threatened the very economic existence of individuals.

The small producer, for example, could survive only if the government preserved 'a free market' by preventing the formation of monopolies, by breaking up those that had been formed and by forcing them into genuine competition.

The Interstate Commerce Commission (1889), the Sherman Anti-Trust Act (1890), the Clayton Act (1914) and the Federal Trade Commission Act (1914) reflected this new effort of the federal government to break up concentrations of economic power and restore a free economic environment in which the small producer could breathe and live.

Inevitably the American in his role as a consumer also began to look to the federal government for protection.

The first major step in this direction followed the publication of Upton Sinclair's *The Jungle* in 1906, a novel revealing the pestilential conditions prevailing in Chicago's stockyards and meat-packing establishments.

Not long thereafter President Theodore Roosevelt induced Congress to pass the Pure Food and Drug Act, which excluded adulterated or misbranded food and drugs from interstate commerce. A second major step, this time at the insistence of the consumers of electrical power, led to the creation of the Federal Power Commission in 1920.

Yet the government's regulatory powers were based on the notion that all that was required was to restore the free market or to correct its notorious abuses. The fundamental assumption that the free market, once revitalized, was itself a sufficient guarantee of economic growth and prosperity was never questioned.

The new regulatory power, therefore, provided no answer to the violent swings between booms and busts which produced thirty major panics and depressions between the founding of the Republic and the first decade of the twentieth century.

As early as the election of 1840 an Administration visibly suffered at the polls because people began to feel that the 'government ought to do something' to revive a depressed general economy. But it was a long time after that before we began to look beyond the 'corrective action of natural forces'.

In successive panics and depressions, despite the prevailing distress, we were content to let the situation work itself out in its own good time.

We reasoned that when wages and prices went down far enough and past debts had been wiped out by some means or other, those who still had money and credit would be lured by low costs and the prospect of high profits to start buying and building again, and thus produce an upswing in the economy.

It took the near collapse of our own economy between 1929 and 1932 to demonstrate the political futility of such thinking. By then, however, we had also had an opportunity to learn that the issue of domestic prosperity was deeply involved in the even larger issue of world peace.

CHAPTER VIII

Our Stake in Freedom Overseas

How did the American Dream relate to the world beyond the oceans? Many early Americans, contrary to modern folklore, believed that the relationship was very close.

'All eyes are opening to the rights of man,' Thomas Jefferson asserted two weeks before his death.

'The light of science,' he said, 'has already laid open to every view the palpable truth that the mass of mankind have not been born with saddles on their backs, nor a favoured few booted and spurred, ready to ride them.'

Here, from the author of the Declaration of Independence himself, was a recognition that we were interdependent with the rest of mankind.

Here was a call to the pursuit of our national objectives beyond our frontier, even before our frontier was closed.

These sentiments were not merely academic. The Greek revolution against the Turks in the 1820's, for instance, tapped a wellspring of fervent approval and aid in America.

At the request of the State of South Carolina, Congress adopted an official resolution praising 'the noble and patriotic struggle of the modern Greeks to rescue the hallowed land of Leonidas and Socrates', hailing 'with pleasure' the independence of Greece.

In January 1827, Congressman Livingston of Louisiana rose to speak in terms not unlike those of their Congressional counterparts 120 years later, when aid to Greece was again on the agenda :

> For myself, I trust to the simple statement that here is a whole nation professing the faith in which we believe, asserting the liberty which we enjoy, contending for them against a merciless and powerful enemy, with a courage not equalled in the heroic ages of their ancestors. . . .

They called upon us for aid, and we have the means to afford it. The will, I trust, is not wanting.

Throughout most of the nineteenth century, however, our sheer national involvement with taming a continent meant that the chief objects of American foreign policy were reducible to two ideas.

The first was to establish national sovereignty over all the land that lay between the Atlantic and Pacific Oceans, north of what is now Mexico, and south of what is now Canada.

The second, in which British and American interests coincided and in which the British fleet therefore served as our unspoken ally, was to preserve the territorial independence of the new nations of the Western Hemisphere from further political encroachments by the colonial nations of Europe.

The United States pursued these two concrete objects with skill and persistence. But by the end of the nineteenth century and beginning with the twentieth, our diplomacy moved from a continental to an oceanic basis. The old and measurable objects – land and security from physical subjugation – began to be displaced by more adventuresome ambitions.

At first, perhaps, this reflected no more than the desire of a dynamic young nation to be recognized as a 'world power'. President McKinley's slogan in the Republican campaign of 1900 after the Spanish-American War was 'Don't haul down the flag!'

But our insistence on holding our recent windfall acquisition of islands in the Pacific expressed something more than a certain aimless turn-of-the-century exuberance.

Indeed our familiar concept of 'Manifest Destiny' soon began to exude a strangely un-American 'smell of empire'.

'Fellow-Americans, we are God's chosen people,' Senator Beveridge of Indiana exclaimed in the Senate in January 1899. 'His power directed Dewey in the East and delivered the Spanish fleet into our hands. His great purposes are revealed in the progress of the Flag. Where the Flag leads we follow, for we know the Hand that bears it onward is the unseen Hand of God.'

But McKinley, Beveridge and the blustering new imperialism were not allowed to go unchallenged by spokesmen closer to the American liberal tradition.

'When you raise the Flag over the Philippine Islands as an emblem of dominion and acquisition,' replied Senator Hoar of Massachusetts, 'you take it down from Independence Hall. I do not agree that the lesson of our first hundred years is that America is to begin the twentieth century where Spain began the sixteenth.'

The American liberal tradition awaited only Woodrow Wilson and our involvement in World War I to reassert itself in a world setting.

In 1914, when the Kaiser's spike-helmeted infantry streamed across Belgium and northern France, the conflict had seemed remote and our interests negligible. But gradually we began to sense the degree to which our national security was linked with that of Britain and France.

For a century the British Navy and the European power balance preserved by British diplomacy had made American isolationism possible. What if this barrier should be destroyed?

In the Jeffersonian tradition, Wilson saw the impending struggle as far more than an effort to redress the European power balance. 'The world,' he said, 'must be made safe for democracy.'

That was America's purpose, and because it was also the purpose of most of mankind, for one happy interval Wilson seemed to speak not only for his fellow Americans, but for his fellow men everywhere who owed allegiance to the Party of Hope.

The American people agreed that it would be a 'war to end wars'. And in the peace that was to come, we would work with others 'to make the world itself at last free'.

We would be 'the champions of the rights of mankind',

including 'the right of those who submit to authority to have a voice in their own governments'.

Indeed, Wilson reminded us that 'America was created to unite mankind'. With this purpose in mind, his 'urgent advice' was for Americans not only to think of America, but in order to be truly American, 'always, also, to think first of humanity'.

As I heard these words as a boy, they stirred me more than any I had ever heard before. They led me to break with the Republican party of my father, and ultimately they led me into public life in the hope that I could somehow help to make the words come true.

Wilson's great objective seemed to me to make sense, to give a moral base to our national and international actions. This was the logical application of the first principles on which our country was founded. This was the extension on a world-wide scale of those truths which we once held self-evident.

Wilson's words rekindled the flame of human idealism that had flickered to near extinction in the stench of the wartime trenches on the Western front.

The proof was in the way French peasants knelt in homage as Wilson's train sped through their countryside.

It was in the way governments, as in Italy, trembled when Wilson went over their heads to appeal to the people.

It was in the way millions in Asia and in Africa straightened up to the new conviction that soon they would no longer be the world's forgotten men.

It may properly be said that America was younger then in her knowledge of world affairs – naïve and youthful and idealistic. That may be so, but in our first entry into the world after more than a century of preoccupation with our internal development, we managed to capture and lift the spirit of humanity.

The new world came to the rescue and liberation of the old not only with tanks and doughboys, but with electrifying ideas. The old world responded, and gave us its heart. As a people, we said through Wilson that what happens to the least of men anywhere, happens to all men everywhere.

We said that those who turn their backs on wrongs they have the power to avert, share in the fault of those who initiate the wrongs themselves.

We said that the highest honour goes to a people who have at hand all the resources for a life of ease, and yet do not withhold sustenance from those who are hard-pressed. We said that in our view, there are no expendable men and nations that can be sacrificed as means to the ends aggressive power sets for itself.

In that hour, America through Wilson stood before the world as a society committed to the Party of Hope in the formidable maze of world politics.

In pursuit of his objective Wilson may have compromised too much in Paris and too little in Washington. Yet on the central question of his time, he was everlastingly right.

Over and over again he warned us that if we rejected his vision and seceded from the emerging world community, we would not only 'break the heart of the world' but that we would pay for our failure in blood.

'There will come, sometime,' he warned us, 'in the vengeful providence of God, another struggle in which not a few hundred thousand fine men from America will have to die, but as many millions as are necessary to accomplish the final freedom of the people of the world.'

Twenty-one years later his prophecy of a Second World War came true as the Nazi Panzer divisions embarked on their savage rush across the Polish plains.

He was proved right because we did not stay with the task of creating the necessary conditions that would have allowed the new war-born democracies of Europe to take deep root and grow.

Instead, the pull of isolationism was too strong. In the United States Senate, a 'little group of wilful men' set out to destroy Wilson's vision and to return us to more familiar paths.

Our entry into the new League of Nations was narrowly blocked, and America tragically turned her thoughts inward, away from her destiny.

Because we refused the challenge, the dominating fact of the First World War came to be the Russian Revolution.

While Wilson was outlining his doomed plans for a world community based on tolerance and co-operation, Lenin was emerging triumphant from the Russian Revolution to proclaim his own version of an upside-down One World of Communism.

In his new world, peace would be achieved by class warfare, freedom would be achieved by dictatorship, the classless society would be achieved by the supremacy of the proletariat, and the 'withering away of the state' would be achieved by making the state omnipotent in all matters.

But in 1920, after the abortive uprisings in Hungary and Germany and the Red Army's defeat before Warsaw, the Soviet Union also withdrew into isolationism, content for a while to foster Communist agitation and united fronts abroad, and to create in Russia a more powerful industrial, military and organizational base. The *world* revolution could wait until conditions became more favourable.

Our failure was not in preventing the rise of Communism in Russia, which was beyond our power. It was in failing to use the interval to create a living partnership with the existing free nations and to support the emergence of others.

The cost of our failure soon became evident. First in Mussolini's Italy, and then more threateningly as Hitler rose to power in Germany, the precepts of democracy were openly repudiated. On the pretext of dealing with revolutionary Communism, the forces of conservatism which should have jealously guarded those precepts made common cause with their own destroyers.

In Fascist Italy and soon in Nazi Germany, the vision of the human community was held up to scorn. To seek it, or even to speak of it in any way, became a crime against the state. The master nation, the master race, was enthroned in its place.

It was inevitable that these forces would dress themselves in military uniforms and march off to war. But all that was far away in Europe, thousands of miles from Akron, Chippewa Falls, Council Bluffs and Fresno.

Here then was the story and the status of the American Dream as our fathers knew it. Successive generations of Americans had steadily contributed the necessary raw materials of vision and effort – the stuff of which dreams and history are made.

In some periods the dream had faltered. In others its fulfilment had been swift and dramatic. In still others we had bided time.

Yet the sum total had been a gradual unfolding of new areas of freedom. Each advance, moreover, could be realistically tested in terms of the progressive rise of a majority of Americans to higher and still higher levels of individual dignity and opportunity.

By October 1929, it seemed as though Americans had lived and written history's greatest success story. To some it may have seemed that America had already become the 'New Eden' of our early nineteenth-century prophets.

We had spanned the continent and created great cities.

We had struggled to extend and protect our basic civil and political liberties against various kinds of deprivation and denial.

We had assimilated tens of millions of immigrants of many different ethnic strains to create a new, identifiably American people.

Through our system of free, all-inclusive, public education, we had wiped out illiteracy, equalized opportunities in the competition of life, and instilled in our boys and girls habits of living suited to democracy.

We had steadily expanded the meaning of economic liberty for all Americans.

For one brilliant but fleeting moment in 1917–19, we had even stirred the world's imagination with a glimpse of the relevance of our American Dream to other lands and people.

Our progress had come in a series of forward surges followed by periods of relaxation. The first two decades of the twentieth century in particular had been filled with turmoil and tension.

The American people wanted repose from old problems and escape from new ones. Warren Harding, Calvin Coolidge and Herbert Hoover and their promises of 'normalcy' reflected this national mood.

What liveliness there was in the 1920's came not from the challenge of new political issues but from prohibition, Al Capone, flagpole-sitting contests and the Charleston; from the Florida land boom, and that inexhaustible source of get-rich-quick millionaires, the New York stock market.

In the midst of this political apathy and surface glitter, few Americans sensed that they were about to be tested profoundly, as was the durability of their democratic society.

PART III

In Pursuit of
Economic Abundance

America is a land of wonders, in which everything is in constant motion and every change seems an improvement. The idea of novelty is there indissolubly connected with the idea of amelioration. No natural boundary seems to be set to the efforts of man; and in his eyes what is not yet done is only what he has not yet attempted to do.

ALEXIS DE TOCQUEVILLE

Democracy in America, 1835

CHAPTER IX

The New Deal Balance Sheet

IN EARLY autumn of 1929, most Americans believed that we had reached a permanent high plateau of prosperity where, every day in every way, things would get better and better.

As a young man I had started a new business in the spring of that year with a small amount of savings, spurred on by the assurances of older businessmen that depressions were forever behind us.

On October 29th, the bottom fell out of the stock market, and our economy drifted rapidly into the most massive depression in American history.

Few men in business or in public life could at first grasp the magnitude of the disaster. Many in the fall of 1929 agreed with Secretary of the Treasury Andrew Mellon, who said : 'I see nothing in the present situation which is either menacing or warrants pessimism.'

Along with thousands of other respected observers, Mr Mellon turned out to be wrong.

Our gross national output dropped steadily from $100 billion to $42 billion in 1932. Farm income slumped seventy per cent. In that year alone thirty thousand businesses went bankrupt. Three-fourths of those which survived were operating in the red.

The Hoover Administration prescribed a course of action that sounds depressingly similar to that which many advocate today : the federal budget must be balanced, not only in prosperous years but in poor years as well, *regardless* of economic or social consequences. There must be an end to public borrowing under any and all conditions, and more vigorous insistence on a 'sound' dollar at whatever cost.

At first such principles had vigorous bipartisan support. Indeed the Democratic platform in the summer of 1932 assailed the budgetary deficits of the Hoover Administration and pledged a new Democratic Administration to 'an immediate and drastic reduction of governmental expenditures, which will accomplish a saving of not less than twenty-five per cent in the cost of the Federal Government and provide for a federal budget annually balanced'.

Even the Democratic Presidential nominee, Governor Franklin D. Roosevelt, who was soon to be accused in some quarters of 'radicalism', joined his party's attack on the 'Republican spendthrifts'.

'The Administration,' he said at Hyde Park on July 30th, 1932, 'has resorted to a type of inflation which has weakened public confidence in our government credit at home and abroad. . . . Let us have the courage to stop borrowing to meet continuing deficits. We must stop the deficits.'

Again on October 19th, Mr Roosevelt said : 'The air is surcharged with Republican deathbed repentances on the subject of economy. But it is too late. . . . I regard reduction in federal spending as one of the most important issues in this campaign.'

The foremost leaders of the business community shared this view. In February 1933, Bernard Baruch told the Senate Finance Committee that 'delay in balancing the budget is trifling with disaster'.

General W. W. Atterbury, President of the Pennsylvania Railroad, agreed. 'I can see no reason,' he told the same committee, 'why the government should not conduct its business during these times in exactly the same way as the individual or corporation should do.'

Myron C. Taylor, Chairman of the United States Steel Corporation, felt likewise : 'If the government balanced its budget, and lived within its income,' he said, 'the depression would quickly disappear.'

These statements were made only one month before Mr Roosevelt took his first inaugural oath. By that time raw materials and foodstuffs had no buyers, plant facilities everywhere lay idle, and fifteen million men – one-third of our labour force – were unemployed.

The dollar, judged by the goods and services it could buy, had never been more 'sound'. The irony was that the sounder it became, the more men were thrown out of work, the more businesses went bankrupt, and the more farms were foreclosed.

Indeed, by the first week of March 1933, the dollar had become so fearsomely sound that it closed every bank in the nation.

On March 10th, 1933, six days after entering the White House, Mr Roosevelt asked the Congress for authority to make good on the drastic governmental economies he had pledged during the election campaign.

The deficits run by the government in the three preceding years, he said, had led to the recent collapse of the banking structure. They had accentuated the stagnation in the economic life of the nation, and had added to the ranks of the unemployed.

National recovery, the President emphasized, depended on strict governmental economy and a balancing of the federal budget.

Mr Roosevelt was promptly granted the power he requested. Cuts were made in the payroll of the federal government and in veterans' benefits. Even the small public works programme begun by Mr Hoover was reduced. The naked, rusting girders of the half-completed Department of Commerce building in Washington stood as a symbol of our national determination to balance the federal budget at all costs.

Yet the budget-balancing policy was fated to overthrow itself by its own irrelevance to the needs of the hour. Looking reality in the face, the new Roosevelt Administration soon shook itself free from the classic economic dogmas which had nearly brought our economy to a standstill.

Within a matter of weeks it shifted gears and launched a series of experimental moves designed to put more money into the hands of the consumers, workers, farmers and businessmen.

The national government assumed responsibility not only for relieving immediate distress but for creating a floor of security below which no American family would be allowed to fall. Mr Roosevelt's confident voice assured millions of radio listeners that their principal enemy was fear, and that fear could be conquered by positive federal action backed by a unified public will.

As the newly created purchasing power spread out across the nation, people began to buy again. Workers returned to their jobs by the hundreds of thousands, then by the millions. Profits grew. Debts began to be paid off. Farm foreclosures were halted.

A succession of imaginative economic measures flowed in a steady stream from the White House, through Congressional Committees, onto the floor of the House and Senate, and finally back to the White House for signature.

They were to include the Home Owners Loan Corporation, the Federal Deposit Insurance Corporation, the Works Progress Administration – then the Public Works Administration – Farm Security Administration, Social Security Administration and the Securities and Exchange Commission.

By the early autumn of 1933 the country had begun to breathe more easily. The corner had clearly been turned.

As the economy revived, the advocates of the Old Order recovered their confidence and with it, their voices. Attacks on Mr Roosevelt and his New Deal grew in vehemence.

The critics complained about the creation of the National Labor Relations Board, formed to adjudicate differences between management and labour as part of the new, federally acknowledged right of labour to organize and bargain collectively.

They complained about the establishment of minimum standards of decency in the matter of hours and wages, designed to eliminate sweatshops.

They complained about the establishment of a social security system to help remove the fear of unemployment and of old age.

They complained about the initiation of a slum clearance programme, designed to help eliminate the causes of crime, disease, delinquency and family demoralization.

They complained about the establishment of the Tennessee Valley Authority, which was to enrich the life of an entire region and open up new possibilities in the realm of democratic government for the whole world to see and emulate.

They even complained about the insurance of bank deposits.

All this was denounced as raw socialism, and as unwarranted government interference with private enterprise.

The American people disagreed. In November 1936, Franklin D. Roosevelt was re-elected by the largest landslide of modern American political history. The only dissenting states were Maine and Vermont.

Yet for all its achievements, and for all the Old Guard's complaints about them, it would be misleading to consider the New Deal an unqualified economic success.

Although its relief expenditures never exceeded four billion dollars annually, the new Administration – to its very great credit – succeeded in establishing a level of minimum decency below which no American family would henceforth be allowed to fall.

But as an offset to this revolutionary accomplishment, there was the bleak fact that as late as 1940 more than eight million Americans, or 14·5 per cent of our constantly expanding working force, were looking for jobs.

Many observers believe that the Administration's failure to complete the task of recovery was due paradoxically to its hesitant acceptance of its own economic philosophy. In 1937, for example, with nine million men still unemployed, it attempted prematurely to balance the budget. The result was the sudden halting of the recovery.

In the jolting recession of 1937–38 which followed, the

national income dropped at the rate of nearly a billion dollars a month.

This experience proved persuasive. In his State of the Union and Budget Message in January 1939, Mr Roosevelt laid down a new economic doctrine for America that constitutes an historic landmark in the development of the public philosophy.

Mr Roosevelt made it plain that as long as there were idle men, idle machines and idle capital, his Administration would henceforth balance its budget only as increases in national income created increases in tax receipts. Never again would he agree to cut necessary expenditures or to increase taxes on consumption and capital expansion when our economy was operating below its capacity.

Although the New Deal failed to meet the full challenge of the Depression, its shortcomings may be explained by the sheer magnitude and newness of the problems that bore down upon it, and by the experimentation it had to undergo before it evolved workable techniques.

Meanwhile on the *credit* side of the historical ledger, the entries were enormous : The New Deal constituted a creative economic and social revolution in the proudest tradition of democratic America. It laid the basis for a new national consensus on economic questions. It saved our system of private ownership and restored the validity of the American Dream.

And by demonstrating to the young men and women of America that their well-being was a prime concern of their government, it braced their morale for the ordeal of war which millions of them were soon to experience.

CHAPTER X

A National Economic Consensus?

By December 1943, the turning point of the Second World War had been reached.

Although the Normandy landings were still six months away, the Allied forces had seized the initiative on almost all fronts. The Nazi armies were steadily retreating in Russia. North Africa had been freed. Sicily had been won. American, British and Canadian divisions had begun their long, frustrating struggle up the Italian Peninsula.

In the Pacific, Allied land and naval forces were winning victories after months of grim setbacks.

On his way home after the first meeting of Allied war leaders in Teheran, where plans were considered for the opening of a second front in Europe, President Roosevelt visited many American military units in the Mediterranean area.

Although he was greeted with intense enthusiasm, what impressed him was the unease with which most G.I.'s faced their postwar prospects. On all sides he was bombarded with questions ringing in a uniformly disturbing key:

'When the war is over will there be good jobs for all of us? Or will we be struggling against the same depressed conditions that our fathers knew?"

'How about my chances of making a go of our family dairy farm in Wisconsin?'

'Will there be a chance for a young man to start a small business or will Big Business have it all its own way?'

On his return to Washington, Mr Roosevelt discussed these questions with me and others with whom he worked closely on economic matters. 'The time has come,' he said, 'for a clear statement of the economic principles which the American people are now ready to accept.'

The result was a memorable message to Congress delivered

on January 11th, 1944. Since it has a direct and immediate relevance to our present situation, the message deserves to be quoted here at some length. In his message proclaiming an 'Economic Bill of Rights' Mr Roosevelt said :

This Republic had its beginning and grew to its present strength under the protection of certain inalienable political rights – among them the right of free speech, free press, free worship, trial by jury, freedom from unreasonable searches and seizures. They were our rights to life and liberty.

As our Nation has grown in size and stature, however – as our industrial economy expanded – these political rights proved inadequate to assure us equality in the pursuit of happiness.

We have come to a clear realization of the fact that true individual freedom cannot exist without economic security and independence. Necessitous men are not free men. People who are hungry and out of a job are the stuff of which dictatorships are made.

In our day these economic truths have become accepted as self-evident. We have accepted, so to speak, a second Bill of Rights under which a new basis of security and prosperity can be established for all – regardless of station, race, or creed.

Among these are :

The right to a useful and remunerative job in the industries, or shops or farms or mines of the Nation;

The right to earn enough to provide adequate food and clothing and recreation;

The right of every farmer to raise and sell his products at a return which will give him and his family a decent living;

The right of every businessman, large and small, to trade in an atmosphere of freedom from unfair competition and domination by monopolies at home and abroad;

The right of every family to a decent house;

The right to adequate medical care and the opportunity to achieve and enjoy good health;

The right to adequate protection from the economic fears of old age, sickness, accident and unemployment;

The right to a good education.

All of these rights spell security. And after this war is won we must be prepared to move forward in the implementation of these rights, to new goals of human happiness and well-being.

I ask the Congress to explore the means for implementing this Economic Bill of Rights – for it is definitely the responsibility of the Congress so to do.

Two years later, America's commitment to Mr Roosevelt's objectives was spelled out by Congress in the Employment Act of 1946, together with the approach by which they could be achieved.

This act should be read as a reminder of our government's responsibility for the well-being of the national economy. Its assumptions are basic to the public consensus which had developed on economic affairs even before 1946.

These assumptions may be briefly stated :

First: The objectives laid down in President Roosevelt's Economic Bill of Rights are accepted as national policy : Every American willing and able to work has a right to employment; every businessman has a right to compete in a free market; every farmer has a right to a reasonable opportunity for profit.

Second: America's mass production economy depends for its balance on American mass consumption. Mass consumption, in turn, implies the presence of effective purchasing power equal in amount to the goods and services currently produced by the nation's economic machinery.

Conversely, if this level of purchasing power is not available, the managers of the instruments of production will lack the effective demand for their products that alone will justify reinvestment of accumulated profits and savings in new plant facilities.

Third: The best way to cure depressions is to avoid them. That means that government must act deliberately as the stabilizing agent in an economy based on the principles of private enterprise.

By the conscious and deliberate use of its constitutional powers as they apply to taxation and expenditures, supplemented by its constitutional powers over monetary and credit policies, the government has the responsibility to maintain a climate of national economic confidence, backed by adequate purchasing power to assure maximum production and employment.

Fourth: In most years this process calls for a balanced budget. And preferably for a budgetary surplus with which to reduce our national debt.

However, in those years when the purchasing power necessary for full employment begins to dry up, the government must put more money back into the economy than it takes out of it in the form of taxes. The resulting unbalanced budget, deliberately brought about in periods of recession or threatened recession, is not a cause but a reflection of a deep-seated unbalance in the economy.

Moreover, a policy of stepped-up governmental outlays for highways, dams, housing, hospitals, schools and other essential national needs, at a time when private enterprise is necessarily curtailing its expenditure, does not reflect a preference for an unbalancd budget. It merely reflects the urgent need to raise the national income by putting idle men, money and machines to work.

As this occurs and as private enterprise is stimulated to expand its production and to absorb the unemployed, the budget can and *should* be brought promptly into balance. Surpluses should be used to lower our national debt, which will thus become a steadily diminishing burden over the years.

This action offsets the danger of an *inflationary* boom on

the economic upswing, just as an unbalanced budget can help counteract a growing *deflation* or recession on the downswing.

Fifth: It is irrelevant to talk about the federal government as though it were an individual, a family or a corporation.

Private institutions must balance their outgo with their income within a reasonable span of years or they do indeed go broke. But the federal government stands on an economic plane of its own, with legal powers that are beyond those that are wielded at the city and state level of government.

It alone has the power within broad limits to make and change the rules of the national economic game according to the needs of the nation as a whole.

It alone accounts for a sufficient portion of our total national spending so that it can by a single decision compensate for fluctuations in our countless unco-ordinated private decisions to spend, save or invest.

Through its paramount power of taxation on a national basis, it alone has the means to regulate the national accumulation and distribution of wealth production.

Lastly, it alone has the power to mobilize the resources of the whole nation for the benefit of all the people in it.

The wide public acceptance of these concepts came to represent a consensus that our two political parties gradually embraced for reasons of their own political survival.

To be sure, during the 1930's most Republican leaders bitterly dissented, and this is enough to explain the successive defeats of their party. But in the 1940's, they began to say that they did not challenge the New Deal programmes or goals as such but only the way the Democrats handled them.

In 1948, after sixteen years in the wilderness, the Republican's candidate for President, the highly realistic Thomas E. Dewey, sounding for all the world like a confirmed New Dealer, seemed to be headed straight for the White House. But when some of his associates blurted out criticisms of the Welfare State, the suspicion grew that he was a liberal front for the discredited Old Guard viewpoint, and his Presidential chances ebbed.

No one ever doubted where Harry Truman stood on the Rooseveltian revolution and he won the greatest upset victory in our political history.

In 1952 Mr Eisenhower avoided Mr Dewey's errors. With his fresh appeal and a series of speeches committing himself and his party to the economic consensus introduced by the previous Administration, he seemed to be the answer that voters longed for.

Weary with crises, eager for fresh political faces, and convinced that the time had come for a change, they eagerly accepted Modern Republicanism at its face value and over-whelmingly voted Mr Eisenhower into office.

CHAPTER XI

Too Many Recessions

DURING the first few years in office the new Administration made a modest effort to carry out its pledge to continue the New Deal while improving its administration. Yet even twenty years of election defeats left the conservative leaders of the Republican party unconvinced.

Therefore, following the election of 1956 the conflict between the economic restrictionists and expansionists, which has characterized our economic history, began again in earnest. It took shape under the spur of two events, which occurred almost simultaneously.

One was the serious disturbance in the American economy which was dimly visible as early as April 1957, but which became unmistakably clear by the early autumn of that year. The second was the extraordinary demonstration of Soviet scientific and industrial capacity provided by the launching of Sputnik in early October.

As winter approached, more and more industrial plant facilities lay idle. More and more raw materials piled up as a glut on the market. And with every passing day more and more men were losing their jobs.

But before we deal with the implications of this recession, it is important to clear up some statistical confusion. Apologists for our present restrictive economic policies stress the sizable rate of expansion of our industrial output as it swings up from the low levels of the most recent recession. They overlook the fact that these increases are calculated from figures that are well below the previously established high levels.

Half the time since 1950 we have been either sliding into a recession or struggling back out of one. The result has been an average annual growth rate that is less than half of our historic expansion – and this at a time when our economy and indeed our entire system is facing an unprecedented challenge.

Three recessions in ten years, the first in 1949, the second in 1953–54, and the third in 1957–58, have cost us nearly $400 billion in goods and services that we could have produced, but didn't. This waste is so colossal that it is difficult for the mind fully to grasp its dimensions.

Moreover, the cost of periodic recessions and a slow average rate of economic growth cannot be measured solely in terms of lost production. When our economy expands slowly over a period of years or not at all, relations between labour and management worsen as each group comes to feel that it can move ahead only at the expense of the other. This situation has become increasingly serious.

Moreover, when jobs become scarce, it is the members of our minority groups who are often the first to be fired, the last to be hired, and who therefore suffer most.

A slow rate of economic growth also curtails the sources of government revenues. This, in turn, leads to further delays in the urgently needed re-examination of our tax structure.

Because our revenue-starved states and local governments are unable to keep up with costs involved in servicing their burgeoning populations, there is pressure for an unhealthy concentration of governmental power in Washington.

Nor is this all. A slow rate of economic growth encourages a creeping isolationism in foreign affairs. It leads us to accept the rationalization that a second-best military establishment is adequate. It leads to political pressures for higher protective tariffs.

It leads many liberal legislators to vote for dangerous slashes in overseas economic programmes which are essential to our national interests on the ground that if a stand-pat Administration tells us we cannot afford to build dams in Idaho, we should retaliate by refusing to build them in Pakistan.

Meanwhile, as we debate our national capacity to grow at the rate we have grown for the last one hundred years, Khrushchev has bluntly laid down the economic gauntlet: 'The Soviet Union,' he said, 'intends to outstrip the United States economically . . . and to surpass the level of production in the United States means to exceed the highest indexes of capitalism.'

Mr Allen Dulles, able head of the Central Intelligence Agency, reminds us of the hard facts lying behind Mr Khrushchev's challenge: Soviet universities are now turning out twice as many qualified scientists and engineers as our own. The overall rate of Soviet industrial expansion for the last seven years has been 9·5 per cent annually. The new Soviet Seven-Year Plan calls for an aggregate industrial increase of 80 per cent by 1965.

'If it is true that our industrial growth in this period will be only two per cent a year,' Mr Dulles concluded, 'the United States will be virtually committing economic suicide.' Mr Dulles might have added *political* suicide as well.

Now let us face a related and equally hard fact. If we fail to match Soviet progress in national productivity and growth, the fault will not lie in any inherent defect in the capitalist system. West Germany, Mexico, Japan, and other capitalist nations are showing rates of growth fully comparable to those of Communist Russia.

Where, then, will the fault lie if we fail to grow in line with our economic potentialities? It will lie squarely on the failure of the American people to insist that their government create the psychological atmosphere and the economic conditions necessary to keep our capitalist system in good working order.

American enterprise will continue to move sluggishly with periodic setbacks, unless we clear our minds of the defeatist attitudes that now block the growth of which we are capable. In the face of the Soviet economic challenge, to re-embrace the discredited theory of scarcity that persisted throughout the 1930's, when many people came to believe that future rapid growth was a practical impossibility, would be tragic.

It was argued then with special emphasis that economic power had become so concentrated through the growth of monopolies that competition would soon disappear, thus putting an outer limit on expansion. Inevitably this would lead to a hardening in the lines of class consciousness, to a pitting of labour against management, and both against the farmer.

Indeed, the new pessimism that was taking shape in American thought in the late 1930's seemed to support the Marxist prophecy that capitalism was doomed by its 'inner contradictions'.

This unbecoming economic pessimism continued to dominate our thinking even after we were drawn into the war by the Japanese attack on Pearl Harbour. Congressional and public reaction to President Roosevelt's State of the Union Message of January 6th, 1942, is a case in point.

In this message the President asked Congress to provide for the production of 45,000 combat planes and six million tons of shipping in the coming fiscal year.

Many of his advisers had previously told him that these goals were impossibly high, especially since only one million tons of shipping had been constructed in 1941. But the 1937 recession had taught the President that our capacity to produce is limited only by our human and natural resources and by our national will. He, therefore, told them to go back and sharpen their pencils.

The production goals which resulted were generally dismissed as a clever propaganda gambit, calculated to impress our enemies, but clearly unattainable in the world of real fact. But the economic restrictionists had again underestimated our capacity.

In 1942 we produced not 45,000 planes but 48,000. Instead of six million tons of shipping, our output was eight million. In that single year, overall industrial production jumped by twenty-two per cent.

And this was only the beginning. By 1944 the number of airplanes produced in America had soared to 96,000 and the amount of shipping to twenty million tons.

By then we had withdrawn almost twelve million of our most active and productive men and women into the armed forces. Yet this had not kept us from creating many new industries and greatly expanding existing ones such as magnesium, synthetic rubber, aircraft and shipbuilding.

By 1945 our gross national product had soared to $213·6 billion while price levels under a complex but effective system of price, wage and rationing controls remained almost stable.

If our production capacity had been as limited as the sceptics assumed it to be, World War II would have been prolonged for several more years, our casualties would have been infinitely more severe, and the American people would have been subjected to severe privation.

What the restrictionists failed to see was that the growth of our economy depends, not on phantom doctrines, but on a combination of two dynamic factors.

First, a set of clear, generally accepted, national objectives.

Second, a democratic leadership free of doctrinaire theory which (a) accepts those objectives, (b) knows that the American people are great builders who build best when they are called upon to build greatly, and (c) creates the economic conditions enabling them to do so.

Yet old concepts die slowly. No sooner had we successfully shown our capacity to meet the economic challenge of war, than new doubts appeared to confuse our planning for a full-production, peacetime economy.

Immediately after the collapse of Japan, Washington was once again overrun with anxious leaders of industry, labour, agriculture and government, who outdid each other in their gloomy prophecies about the future.

Our war-created plant capacities, many of them told us, would go largely unused. Prices must be set high enough to enable high profits to be made with twenty to forty per cent of our capacity idle.

We would have to adjust ourselves again, they asserted, to substantial continuing unemployment as the inescapable price for freedom of enterprise and price stability.

As a member of the War Production Board involved in planning the nationwide reconversion to a peacetime economy, I shall not soon forget the impact of these dire prophecies on the Board's thinking. It was only by a very great wrench of the spirit that we managed to keep our perspective.

Yet how could we have planned for anything less than a rapidly expanding fully productive economy?

With our increased productivity and greatly expanded work force, to go back to 1939 levels of production would mean that fifteen to twenty million workers would be without jobs.

The American people had experienced full production and a rising standard of living while fighting a global war. How could they be expected meekly to accept mass unemployment as a 'normal' condition of a peacetime economy?

So we proceeded to base our postwar economic goals on the premise that never again could the American people accept the inevitability of unfulfilled needs side by side with idle machines, idle men and idle capital.

In 1946 I mustered the confidence to write an economic primer called *Tomorrow Without Fear*. In it I laid down a peacetime gross national production goal of $200 billion by 1948.

For this I was promptly denounced as a visionary. But events soon proved that I had lacked the vision to set our goal sufficiently high.

Within a short time after V-J Day, we were operating at full capacity. A switchover of twelve million veterans to peacetime jobs was accomplished with scarcely a ripple.

At no time during the whole reconversion period did unemployment rise above 2·5 million. What did rise dramatically was the gross national product. By 1948 it reached $225 billion – at 1946 prices – ten per cent more than my 'visionary' estimate.

I am deeply convinced that this experience is relevant for us today, when we have again lowered our economic sights to the most minimal national goals.

Why has our economy not grown faster in these last six years? Why have we undergone a series of recessions, with many gloomy economic analysts already warning of still another in 1961 or 1962?

The answer, I believe, lies in the timidly restrictive policies under which we have been operating since 1953.

CHAPTER XII

Opposing Theories of Economic Growth

IN this election year, the debate over economic policy will almost certainly become highly partisan. It is important, therefore, to lay down the prospective lines of argument as fairly and honestly as we can before we are swept up in a hurricane of charges and countercharges.

The authors of our present economic policies in the Treasury Department, Federal Reserve Board and Council of Economic Advisers are honourable, public-spirited men.

Like their Democratic predecessors, they accept the institution of private property as the take-off point for our national economic effort. They agree that the political order must have the task of maintaining the frame of liberty in which a separate economic order based largely on private decisions and choices can organize the production and distribution of goods and services.

They agree that government must also have the right to monitor that part of our productive plant which directly affects the interest of the people as a whole with appropriate deference to the rights of ownership and management.

And finally, with varying degrees of enthusiasm, they agree that the government must undertake those essential public projects which are beyond the means of an individual or a group of individuals.

I believe their perspective has become dangerously distorted, however, by a mistaken approach to the question of inflation. As they see it, a sustained high rate of economic growth and a rampant inflation are but two sides of the same coin. According to their view, a stable economy can be assured in two interrelated ways.

One is by higher interest rates that will make the money and credit necessary to expansion more costly and hence less available. The other is by federal policies designed deliberately to restrict the government's own contribution to an expanding economy.

This, they admit, often means the postponement or elimination of domestic and foreign projects of great urgency, which, with our economy operating in low gear, can only be paid for through high taxes or an unbalanced budget.

These financing methods, however, are wholly unacceptable. Higher taxes, they say, would 'shake confidence', discourage private incentive, and so retard private investment of capital.

An unbalanced federal budget leading to increased government borrowing for slum clearance, schools, hospitals and road building is also unacceptable because, by increasing the national debt, they assert it would also 'shake confidence', in addition to 'saddling future generations with crushing burdens'.

Worse still, they tell us, it would lead to an inflation which would destroy all stable units of economic measurement, erode the value of savings, and reduce the standard of living of all who live on pensions and insurance policies and all whose salaries do not readily lend themselves to cost-of-living adjustments.

Finally, they believe that unless government in general reduces its activities it will destroy the character of the American people by undercutting their 'traditional habits of self-reliance'.

In their robustly sincere presentation of this economic theory of stability achieved through stagnation, many Administration leaders admit that the curtailment of federal programmes can have a number of regrettable by-products.

Yet it is alleged this situation must be squarely faced and accepted as one of the cruel and unalterable facts of our current national experience. If we were to do all that admittedly needs to be done without regard to its effect on the price structure, the larger cruelty, they assert, would be the inevitable destruction or abandonment of our whole economic system of free enterprise.

In fact, say these Administration spokesmen, the Cold War

aim of the Soviet Union is precisely that. It is to force us to adopt 'reckless spending' policies which will lead to the collapse of America from within and thereby give the Communists a cheap and bloodless victory. The outcome of the whole Cold War, therefore, depends on our willingness to sacrifice growth for stability.

Although I disagree vigorously with this economic analysis, I respect the integrity and the conviction of the Secretary of the Treasury, the Chairman of the Federal Reserve Board and other Administration leaders who accept it.

But when it comes to the swarm of corporation executives and conservative politicians who have been clambering on their bandwagon, I confess to supreme scepticism.

Is it a coincidence that these men who now oppose housing, school construction and similar programmes as 'inflationary' are the very same individuals who have consistently fought these programmes over the last twenty-five years?

In the 1930's and 1940's they opposed adequate water resource development, housing and school construction on different grounds: we already had enough, or the American people could not afford to do more, or even if they could, it was not the federal government's responsibility to do anything about it.

Politically speaking, this proved to be a losing game. Had the time, therefore, not come for a flank attack?

Why not pay homage to reclamation, housing and educational goals and even accept theoretically the government's role in these and other such fields? Then the actual proposals could be fought on the ground that they will lead to a 'runaway inflation' that will be 'the ruin of every widow and pensioner from coast to coast'.

These grim warnings from diehard advocates of the Old Order have a doubly dubious ring when we remember their position on the question of inflation in the critical war and postwar years when the danger was infinitely more acute.

From its inception in 1941, groups such as the National Association of Manufacturers fought the wartime Economic Stabilization Programme with a reckless disregard for rising prices and rents. The most effective political voice supporting their views came from the respected Senator Robert Taft of Ohio. In hearings before the Senate Banking and Currency Committee in 1943, he told me time and again that the best we could hope for was to keep the cost of living index from rising more than ten per cent a year.

Senator Taft proved to be wrong. The wartime inflation control programme which he and his supporters fought so bitterly limited the total rise in consumer prices and rents to an average of only three per cent in the period of intense inflationary pressures between May 1943 and the surrender of Japan in August 1945.

But these men remained blind to the dangers. During the switch from wartime to peacetime production when the pressures for high prices still remained explosive they redoubled their efforts to eliminate all controls.

As Director of Economic Stabilization in the spring of 1946 I and many others warned that the premature dismantling of the anti-inflationary programme would bring about a really serious price inflation. We stressed that such a development would create new burdens for every family in the country, increase our national debt and make a mockery of the savings and pension plans on which millions of veterans and others were counting.

Nevertheless, in June 1946, short-sighted business lobbyists and their Congressional spokesmen succeeded in demolishing the legislation which for four different years had enabled us to keep inflation in check. As a result, our homeward-bound veterans were greeted by a cost of living rise of seventeen per cent in six months. By November 1948, the increase had soared to thirty-two per cent.

In the spring of 1948, with the cost of living still rising at nearly one per cent *monthly*, the conservative leaders in

Congress succeeded in pushing through a major tax cut over President Truman's veto, thereby putting more money in circulation and adding fresh fuel to the inflationary fires.

At that time our federal budget showed a surplus of $8·4 billion. Here was the opportune time to use that surplus to reduce our national debt. But conservative leaders in Congress, with their eyes firmly fixed on the fall election, chose to increase the inflationary forces which many of these same individuals now profess to fear.

Therefore, an objective look at the record of the past fifteen years leads largely to one simple conclusion : the newly voiced concern of many Old Guard spokesmen over inflation is nothing more and nothing less than a massive effort to achieve through a flank attack what they have previously failed to achieve through direct action – the blocking of essential national legislation in housing, school and hospital construction and in other areas where federal action alone can meet our national needs.

This effort constitutes a bold and, I believe, a politically reckless attack on the new economic consensus which the last three decades has brought into being. Long before the votes are cast in November 1960, its real objective should have become fully apparent to the American people.

However, the hypocrisy shown today over inflation by many professional hand-wringers should not lead us to forget that inflation itself is a cruel destroyer. After World War I, inflation in Europe helped wipe out the middle class. It paved the way for Fascism and Communism and set the stage for World War II.

As wartime Administrator of the Office of Price Administration and as postwar Director of Economic Stabilization, with control over prices, rents, wages and production priorities, I am deeply conscious of what inflation can do.

I do not agree with those who say that we must accept a modest inflation as an unavoidable but necessary evil. It is all evil and all our ingenuity, public and private, must be employed to see that inflationary pressures are held firmly in check.

Yet the key economic questions still remain to be asked : How can we maintain a high sustained rate of national growth with a stable price level? How can we keep all of our people at reasonably satisfying jobs, with a feeling of personal security and expanding dignity and opportunity?

In the 1930's and 1940's the American people came to see that these economic and social goals were practical and attainable. In 1946 Congress wrote them into the Employment Act by a heavy bipartisan vote.

Yet today, this confident, affirmative approach to America's future is again being challenged by the same economic restrictionists who fought it in the days of Roosevelt and Truman. The fact that they are now marching under a new banner should fool no one.

Now let us consider the economic theory of the economic expansionists who believe that our present national policies are not only timid but misguided.

They charge that these policies reflect the same outmoded notions that have so often upset our economy or retarded its growth in the past.

They reject the scare talk about the 'crushing burden of the federal debt our children's children will have to bear'. They also reject current characterization of vital government expenditures 'as waste', or as being destructive of our national character.

All debts, both public and private, they remind us, are passed along from one generation to the next, just as all assets, both public and private, are handed down from one generation to the next.

If there were no debts, there would be no banks or insurance companies. And without these institutions there would be no credit with which to build new factories and homes, or to finance the purchase of automobiles and house furnishings.

It is good for people to save. It is also good that others should borrow these savings and put them to productive use. Debts and obligations of various kinds are but the other side of investment.

Indeed, if we ever tried to liquidate all our debts or even any substantial fraction, we would precipitate a crisis as severe as the one in 1929–33. It was the forced liquidation of debts in those years that produced the near-total collapse of our economy.

Why denounce a public authority when it borrows and puts to use otherwise idle funds for the construction of roads, dams, bridges, schoolhouses, hospitals, the tools of national defence – and a host of other things that are of vital importance to the community but which cannot be provided by private enterprise?

Are these additions to our national wealth or well-being more 'wasteful' than corporate borrowing to finance plant expansion or private borrowing through mortgages to build a new home?

As for the destruction of 'character': we can never be sufficiently concerned about the dignity and rights of the individual citizen. But the most basic right of all these rights is the right to live, free of any debasing environment at home, or the fear of physical subjugation or destruction by a hostile foreign power.

Hungry stomachs do not build character – especially not when it is known that there are vast, undisposable farm surpluses on hand.

Slums do not build character – especially not when much of our construction industry is idle or working part time.

Exposure to disease does not build character – especially not when it is known that advances in medical science could provide remedies, if only they could be adequately financed.

Lack of modern schooling does not build character – especially not when schooling is now essential to any boy or girl who means to enter the competitions of life on an equal starting basis with his neighbour.

It is inconceivable that we can preserve our free institutions in America – and the dignity of our people along with them – if the only way to remain solvent is to stand still.

As fairly as I can state them, these then are the arguments and counter-arguments between our economic restrictionists and expansionists. We shall hear them presented in varying forms, moods and degrees of responsibility in the months that lie ahead.

CHAPTER XIII

Inflation and the Interest Rates

THE thoughtful citizen must judge between these alternative lines of argument. If he is to judge the case well, he needs to know the material facts which bear upon it.

For instance, is our federal debt actually running away from us?

The answer is a firm negative.

There is no doubt that total American debt – public and private – has increased in the past years. Since 1945 local and state debt has risen four hundred per cent and private debt three hundred per cent.

But in this same period our *federal* debt has increased only five per cent. In 1945 the figure stood at $279 billion. This corresponded roughly to $2,000 for every man, woman and child in the country, adjusted to 1958 prices.

In the fall of 1959 the nation's debt stood at $285 billion. This came to a little over $1,600 for each person in the country – or $400 per person less in 1958 prices than it was in 1945.

Yet this is but a part of the story. Everyone knows that a

private debt of $10,000 is less of a burden to a man earning $15,000 than to one earning $5,000. So it is with our *national* debt.

Since 1945 our gross national product has more than doubled. Thus we are far better able to carry the national debt these days than we were then.

Moreover, all of the debt increase that has occurred could have been avoided if we had been willing to set aside politics and reduce our federal debt when such opportunities presented themselves, as in 1948.

If we turn from the myth of a 'runaway' federal debt to the fear of a 'runaway' inflation, we find that the Administration has once again been basing its policies on factual error.

We all agree that prices are too high. We must do all we can to bring them down. Yet the recent increases have been well below, not above, our long-term averages.

In the decade since 1948, we have undergone increases in wholesale prices averaging 1·3 per cent yearly. This is slightly more than half the average annual rate of 2·5 per cent in wholesale prices since 1900, a period which includes two world wars. As this is written in the autumn of 1959, we can look back on the longest period of price stability in twenty years; it stretches back to March 1958.

Many economic restrictionists hold union labour responsible for whatever price rises have occurred. The phrase 'wage-price inflation' is calculated to link labour unions with the major guilt.

Certain labour unions may, indeed, have acted irresponsibly by pushing wages at a faster pace than increases in productivity or minimum earning requirements would indicate. This is regrettable. So are the wasteful, make-work varieties of labour featherbedding which needlessly raise production costs in many industries.

But let us not indict the fifteen million members of organized labour for recklessly pushing up prices without first examining the facts.

Corporation salaries and dividends have often risen more sharply. Moreover, increases in labour output per hour due to automation and improved techniques have very nearly balanced out the wage rate increases. Factory efficiency has risen thirty-three per cent over the last eight years. This means that the average *cost* of labour per unit of production has gone up far less than most people think.

Even in those industries where increased productivity has lagged behind wage increases, the gap has been much too small to justify the bitterly unfair and divisive attacks that have been launched against the American labour movement as a whole.

It is equally hypocritical and unfair to use the small gap between increased wages and increased productivity to justify price increases like those in the steel industry, for instance, where prices have risen from $54 a ton in 1945 to $155 a ton in 1959.

In the summer of 1959, with its profits after taxes running at a rate of more than a billion dollars annually, the steel industry faced an opportunity for great economic statesmanship. A $10 per ton cut in prices, with the understanding that wages would remain where they were, would have done wonders for the American people and their economy.

In early August I strongly urged the Administration, which has expressed such concern over inflation, to press for such a reduction. Yet this opportunity, and I believe responsibility, was ignored.

Let us not forget that the Great Depression was caused by the maldistribution of our national income and the resulting lack of purchasing power.

Between 1920 and 1929 wages rose only ten per cent while the average output per worker for each hour of effort rose seventy-five per cent. During this period farm income dropped by one-third, while consumer prices remained steady. Income and corporation taxes were very low.

As a result, by 1929 nearly forty per cent of our national

income was going to five per cent of our people. With the general public unable to buy the goods our factories were capable of producing, the collapse was inevitable.

Today, modern science is making possible even greater miracles in factory efficiency. Output per worker grows at an average of three to four per cent annually. Each year our national work force is increased by more than a million men and women.

Automation will bring increasing complexities. And to it will soon be added the extraordinary new industrial force of atomic energy. If there is to be a market for all we are capable of producing, wages must rise as worker productivity rises or prices must be reduced correspondingly. Yet the economic restrictionists do not yet appear to have learned this fundamental economic lesson.

The reasons for our slow growth in recent years are many and complex. But at the heart of the matter lies an economic miscalculation of gargantuan proportions. I refer to the deliberate policy of raising interest rates in order to slow down production and expansion on the assumption that this is the only practical way to avoid inflation.

As taxpayers in the fiscal year 1960, we will spend $8·5 billion in interest charges to carry our national debt. In 1946, when our national debt was only slightly smaller, the interest cost was $4·2 billion less.

This difference would have been more than enough to finance all the 'inflationary' programmes of urban development, public housing, hospital and school construction and medical research that are being seriously considered by the 86th Congress.

The same dangerously mistaken tight money policy that added this extra load on the federal tax system has also added substantially to the tax load of local and state governments which already had been overstrained by the need to expand local services for our exploding population.

For instance, over the last six years the increased interest costs for a twenty-year mortgage on a million-dollar school are close to $200,000, most of which must be paid out of local taxes on over-burdened real estate.

When we add the effect of soaring interest payments on our greatly expanded transcontinental highway programme, our $42 billion defence programme, and the cost of government in general, we can see that our 'anti-inflationary' high interest rates have added many billions of dollars unnecessarily to our taxes.

Nor are the burdens of this mistaken high interest rate policy confined to *public* programmes. This policy has had a particularly savage impact on people of moderate and small incomes.

If a wealthy man, for example, buys a Cadillac, he does not usually have to pay for it on the instalment plan. He can pay cash and avoid interest. If he buys a $100,000 home, he may pay cash also, and thus avoid the increased mortgage payments.

It is the middle- and low-income families who bear the major brunt of high interest rates.

If such families buy a 'low-priced' car under an instalment plan, the increase since 1953 in the carrying charge is nearly $200. The same proportionate increase enters into the cost of every refrigerator, washer and vacuum cleaner bought on time.

The obvious effect is to slow the sales for these products, which leads to a reduction in the output of the industries that manufacture them and hence to unemployment.

High interest rates hit the home building industry with a particularly heavy impact. The increase from 4·5 per cent to six per cent interest on a twenty-five-year, $10,000-home mortgage adds nearly $2,000 to the total cost of the house. This is one major reason why the rate of home construction has lagged so far behind the needs of our expanding population.

Finally, increased interest costs bear heavily on farmers and small businessmen, who, in the nature of their operations, face the need for very frequent refinancing.

By deliberately allowing interest rates to rise, the Administration has placed a substantial burden on all of us as tax-payers, businessmen and consumers. Viewing the economy as a whole, the total increase in interest costs since 1953 is estimated to be twelve billion dollars. This is slightly less than the total value at the farm of all agricultural produce grown in 1959.

Yet this colossal sum total of *additional* interest has not produced a single extra house or school or automobile or Polaris submarine that could not have been produced under the low interest rates which had been in effect for nearly a generation.

It is my strongly held conviction that the principal economic danger we now face is not inflation, but our slow rate of growth compounded by our disturbing recent history of recurring recessions. Temporary bursts of economic activity such as the one we are enjoying as this book goes to press cannot wash out the waste of previous slumps.

Our primary national objective must be to speed up and *sustain* the growth of our economy, prevent recessions, and do both without increasing prices.

I am convinced that one of the primary tasks of the new Administration that takes office in January 1961, should be to meet the question of high prices head on.

In peacetime the government cannot and should not assume a direct price control role. But it can and must take the lead in creating a new mood in management-labour relations that not only accepts the need for price 'stability' but sets the stage for downward price adjustments wherever possible.

We must learn how to translate much of our increasing industrial efficiency into lower prices that will assure full production, full employment, and a stronger competitive position for American products in world trade.

To achieve sustained economic expansion, every citizen must have a chance for useful and remunerative employment. His production will then add to the total output. It represents part of our national growth.

There never was a time when such employment was more easily provided for than now, for the American people were never before faced with so many urgent tasks.

Only if we resume our national economic expansion with reasonable prices can our people buy what they need. Only then can our government support without economic strain the many projects at home and abroad that are vital to our national interests.

When this question of economic growth was first debated in the 1930's and later in the 1940's sharp partisan disagreement was inevitable. A generation later many advocates of the restrictionist economic philosophy have seized upon the diversionary issue of inflation to challenge the consensus.

Yet as the facts are made clear those advocates of the Old Order who still insist that idle men, machines and capital are the price we must pay for national solvency are again likely to have the worst of the argument.

Let us consider, then, some of the public policies which are required to assure a sustained high rate of national growth without inflation.

CHAPTER XIV

The Economic Framework for Expansion

'ECONOMIC stabilizers,' such as Social Security, minimum wages, and unemployment compensation, introduced during the 1930's over bitter opposition from conservative leaders, have almost eliminated the possibility that we shall again see a major economic collapse along the lines of 1929.

Although we have reason to be thankful for this, our task of social invention is far from complete. We must still find ways to do three additional things simultaneously.

First, we need to remove the grounds for the recessions that have now hit us three times in the last ten years alone, at a total cost of $400 billion in lost national production.

Second, we need to step up our annual rate of economic expansion well beyond the level of the two per cent average to which it has been confined in recent years.

And third, we need to keep this expansion proceeding on an even course, without inflationary or deflationary excesses and within the context of a free competitive economy.

Can all three of these objectives be reached simultaneously? The difficulties are formidable. Yet a bipartisan body of expert opinion strongly believes that they can.

The broad agreement between the Democratic Advisory Council views and those of the Special Committee of the Rockefeller Brothers Fund is particularly reassuring. This nonpartisan accord covers not only the urgent need of mastering our present economic difficulties, but our clear ability to do so.

The Rockefeller Brothers Economic Report strongly rejects the present average annual growth rate on the ground that it cannot provide sources of tax revenue to cover even a low rate of governmental expenditures on indispensable programmes.

The Report even rejects an average growth rate of four per cent on the ground that while it would yield 'just enough' tax revenues to cover the projected low rate of federal expenditures, it would not allow for any expansion in public programmes while preserving a balanced budget.

The desirable and attainable growth rate is put by the Rockefeller Report at five per cent annually. Projected to the mid-1960's, this would mean a gross national product of $707 billion, which is fifty per cent higher than the estimated gross national product for 1959.

The Democratic Advisory Council is only slightly more cautious in its projection. Although it agrees that a five per cent growth rate is desirable, it puts the immediately attainable growth rate at a little over four per cent.

Let us now examine a course of action which I believe will make such sustained expansion possible without inflation.

The first requisite, as we have seen, is to make sure that the purchasing power is available to buy all the goods and services that our industry and our manpower, working at capacity or near capacity, can produce. This purchasing power must be provided by three different groups of buyers, or as some would have it – 'spenders'.

First, there are the business 'spenders'. Each year corporations and merchants large and small spend billions on industrial expansion, inventories, new equipment and buildings. These expenditures are vital to our national growth.

Second are the family spenders. Each year all of us, as consumers, spend all or part of our wages, salaries and dividends for food, clothing, travel, movies, automobiles, washing machines, permanent waves, books, TV sets, radios, houses and an endless variety of items which the imagination and productiveness of our economy provides.

Third are the greatly maligned government spenders – federal, state and local. Each year, and in varying amounts, our governmental departments and agencies invest many billions in schools, hospitals, roads, bridges, irrigation projects, police departments, fire departments, and our Army, Navy and Air Force.

Each of these three groups may change the pattern as well as the amount of its buying from year to year. But if we are to have steady, healthy expansion, the total amount they spend must be sufficient to absorb all the goods and services we are capable of producing.

The problem, therefore, is to strike and maintain a balance between these three groups which will insure total production and employment at high sustained levels, and stimulate the steady expansion of our productive capacity.

Now since ours is a private enterprise economy, the role of the businessman is of special, key importance. Let us therefore consider the practical problems he faces as he seeks to keep his workers fully employed, to expand and modernize his plant and play his dynamic role in helping to create a more abundant America.

Under present conditions, every businessman faces two critically important questions.

First, can he maintain an efficient operation that will enable him to turn out products which he can sell at competitive prices, thus assuring his survival in a competitive market?

On this question he cannot properly go to his government for help. In a system of democratic capitalism, the normal risks of competition must be run by the businessman himself.

The second risk he faces is in many ways much more formidable. Will the market – which means the necessary mass purchasing power – be available to keep the industry of which he is a part operating at capacity or at a near capacity basis?

Every businessman knows that recessions, great or small, have occurred with monotonous regularity. Will the next one drive him into bankruptcy regardless of his efficiency and hard work?

In view of all we know about the workings of the modern economy, the risk that the market will not be there to absorb his production is in large measure an unnecessary risk. It can and must be removed or greatly modified. This is an essential function of our national government.

Now, the very mention of federal economic action still causes alarm in some circles. Let's not, however, lose our perspective.

The federal government is *our* government. As long as we fulfil our roles as intelligent citizens there is no reason to be afraid of it. Moreover, if we are unprepared to accept enough government, we will surely end up with too much.

This may seem paradoxical, but it is nevertheless true. For if we refuse to allow our government to help us solve essential problems, the unsolved problems will overtake us, and in the ensuing crisis we will be obliged to call up our government to do far more than would have been necessary had we taken adequate steps sooner.

There is never any need, except in wartime, for our federal government in Washington to issue direct orders to every corporation, business and family, telling them when and what they can buy and sell and for what price. Freedom of direct choice must be preserved to the letter. This lies at the heart of our system of free enterprise.

What the government must do, consistent with free enterprise, is to establish a practical, attainable set of national goals and to manage its own expenditures and its control over credit and money supply so that the necessary purchasing power will always be available to keep the economy in balance.

Nor is it an impossible task. We now have enough experience handling our monetary policy, our tax policy and our regulatory authority to provide the purchasing power necessary to move all or very nearly all of the goods we are capable of producing.

Once our government begins to fulfil this essential function, it will give every competent businessman a bracing assurance. Thereafter he can safely expand his plants, increase his production and employment, improve his products and set prices low enough to assure the flood of buying necessary for capacity volume and increasing profits. This will help create steady national growth.

Let us now turn to the argument that we cannot employ all Americans who need and want work without causing a dangerous inflation.

There are two kinds of inflation. One is the classical type in which there is too much money chasing too few goods. This was the case after the Second World War and during the first part of the Korean War.

The other is a relatively new type of inflation in which prices in a few tightly controlled semi-monopolistic industries are raised regardless of market considerations. Professional economists call these 'administered prices'.

What makes this type of inflation particularly destructive to a healthy rate of growth is the fact that it often develops into a kind of vicious circle.

When business is slow, prices are raised to create larger profits from limited volume. Thus in 1958 both the steel and automobile industries raised their prices although they were operating at less than sixty per cent capacity.

When business picks up, the soaring profits which result from these higher prices stimulate demands for higher wages. Once granted, the higher wages are then used to justify *further* price increases.

Inflation of this sort obviously does not originate in the classic situation in which there is too much money and too few goods. It exists in the face of unused plant facilities and idle workers and presents us with a new kind of problem.

A tight-money policy with higher interest rates is useful in controlling a demand inflation, but clearly it cannot control an administered inflation where price levels are established without regard for the amount of money and credit in circulation.

As long as there are a substantial number of idle machines and idle workers, credit should be *easier* and not tighter. This means that interest rates should be kept down as we kept them down between 1930 and 1953. This will greatly reduce business and government costs, and it will stimulate necessary capital investment.

However, the new government which we elect in 1960 will not be able to switch policies overnight. The policies of the last few years have created a difficult and complex situation in government financing which is too technical to examine here.

Let us remember, however, that we were able to finance our extraordinary industrial expansion in World War II under the most acute inflationary pressures with interest rates far lower than those of today.

The Federal Reserve Board bought whatever government bonds were required to keep the bonds selling at par. Then to keep this extra capital from being used by the banks as a basis for additional inflationary loans, it ordered the banks to hold a high level of reserves against the loans that had already been made.

This tested two-step procedure was repealed by our present government. As a result interest rates have moved to the highest levels in forty years.

A primary task of the new Administration that takes office in January 1961, will be to restore this policy and thereby reduce interest rates to normal levels. This will save billions of dollars for the taxpayer, reduce the cost of new housing and all goods bought on time, and encourage the building of new plants and the modernization of old ones.

At the same time steps should be taken to prevent or control the administered price increases in the few key monopolistic industries to which I have referred.

One difficulty now is that we do not have the full facts. In the conflict over steel prices and wages in the summer of 1959, for instance, the air was blue with conflicting statistics.

Management charged that 'radical union leaders' were trying to dry up its profits and send it into bankruptcy. Labour charged that the 'steel barons' were striving to destroy the unions. The result was an embittering impasse which cost us millions of tons of steel, and slowed down our recovery.

In such situations wouldn't it be helpful if a panel of respected objective citizens could listen to each side air its position in public and then give the public the *real* facts on which it could make its judgment?

The conclusion reached by the panel need not be binding on either management or labour. But an objective finding of facts would surely have a persuasive influence on both of them.

The success of such procedures would, of course, depend upon the responsible and objective manner in which wage-price hearings were held and the amount of publicity attending the results. Legislation now before Congress would make such hearings mandatory in basic industries such as steel which affect the entire economy.

Another urgent requirement for an expanding economy without inflation is a skilfully balanced tax system that will encourage growth and help assure the purchasing power needed for capacity production.

The present general corporation tax of fifty-two per cent on all corporate profits keeps smaller companies from ready access to capital they need to develop new products, to conduct research and to develop the new markets they must have if they are to compete successfully with the giants. Some form of relief should be provided, perhaps on a graduated basis allowing more favourable rates for small business.

Some sectors of industry in areas where unemployment persists should be given added tax incentives to encourage them to modernize plants and to build new ones. In many capitalist nations industries which are considered essential to general growth are allowed to write off such investment for tax purposes much faster than in America.

An improved manufacturing plant would itself permit lower costs and prices and at the same time increase purchasing power.

The Soviet Union, with a gross national product less than half our own, is investing more new capital in new plants and machinery than we are. The Soviet machine tool industry is now *double* ours.

These are sobering facts to which there is only one practical answer. The Administration elected in 1960 must face up to its responsibility for assuring a sustained growth rate of between four and five per cent annually without recessions and without inflation. Once this is accomplished, new economic horizons will quickly open up to us.

To illustrate what we can do, let us consider the situation which might then face the newly elected 87th Congress in the spring of 1961 as it tackles the budget of the fiscal year 1962.

With a four per cent annual growth rate, our rapidly increasing work force, marginal unemployment at a practical minimum of two million, reduced interest rates, and tax loopholes closed, our federal tax income could be close to ninety billion dollars – twelve billion more than in fiscal year 1960.

Some of our regular housekeeping costs would also be higher to take care of our rising population. But lower unemployment compensation commitments and lower expenses for the farm programme would compensate for these increases.

Under such circumstances Congress could adequately meet our defence and foreign economic assistance needs, expand our construction programmes in housing, urban renewal, schools, dams, highways and reclamation, balance the budget, and either cut our national debt or reduce taxes.

This is not political whimsy. This is the hard arithmetic of sustained economic growth.

And only through such growth can we be assured a prosperous, abundant America, with rapidly disappearing poverty, with opportunities for everyone, with lessening tensions between labour and management, in a world in which we are boldly playing our part as a great and influential democratic leader.

Now let us turn briefly to some of the domestic objectives which under such circumstances would be readily obtainable.

CHAPTER XV

Quality and Quantity of Progress

As we have seen, America's potential for growth is far greater than that of any other nation at this point in history. If we but rally our will and intelligence, the dynamism of the American people and of our economic system will enable us to break out of our present rut, avoid costly periodic recessions, and resume our normal steady growth.

This leads us to a formidable question: What direction should our further economic development take?

Professor John Kenneth Galbraith and others have recently been conducting an important public discussion of this question.

They observe that, in the past, our major emphasis has been on the quantity of our economic output and not on the quality of our values, and that we have been so successful that we are now members of an 'affluent society'. Yet by virtue of our emphasis on quantity, we have failed to concern ourselves as much as we should with the quality of American life.

The result is a widespread public frustration and aimless grasping for material gain that undermines our national character and distorts our values. The effects can be seen in the social disorder which shows itself in the rising rates of juvenile delinquency, crime and divorce.

Such a situation, these critics believe, calls for a fundamental shift of energies, with less emphasis on the quantity of our economic output and more on the quality of our national life.

This argument has a great deal of validity and *The Affluent Society* may be remembered as one of the most influential books of our time. Yet for purposes of this discussion, two additional points should be considered.

First, almost everyone recognizes that the quantitative challenge has by no means been met. In every big city in the nation, a large part of the population is still living in slum areas or in areas that are fast becoming slums. Office buildings are often shoddy, streets are traffic-choked, parking areas over-crowded, and public transportation systems are snarled or in a state of advanced decay.

If we visit with responsible officials in these cities, we hear melancholy recitals of facts and figures about the lack of medical care, the lack of decent schools, the lack of adequate playgrounds, cultural opportunities, police and fire protection, even the lack of proper nutrition.

We Americans have by no means satisfied, or even begun to satisfy, our quantitative needs. Most of us are not yet as affluent as we like to think. Many of us are not affluent at all. Indeed one out of every five American families is still living on less than $2,000 a year.

The second point is that, much as we may wish for it, we cannot legislate quality in a direct way as we legislate a system of minimum wages.

This is not to say that the quality of American life is not a concern of government. It is and should be one of its central concerns. Indeed, it is both necessary and proper that our governmental as well as private agencies advance programmes that will improve the opportunity of every family for a fuller life.

This objective includes decent housing, a better education for all our children, and for the specially talented, all the higher education they can usefully absorb. In addition, our federal government can and should support private agencies and local governments to help expand community *cultural* facilities – symphonies, operas, libraries, museums, historic buildings, recreation and sports.

Still, the primary responsibility of a democratic government in such matters is to help establish a general climate in which our society itself can voluntarily improve its quality.

Within that climate, the better cultivation of the arts and sciences, and the public's increased capacity to discriminate between the first-rate and the second-rate, must be the work primarily of community leaders, foundations, the press, churches, universities and the like.

Over the years these non-governmental sources can and must generate new forces and pressures which will stir our government to adopt the active programmes that will help further to improve the quality of our society.

A fuller discussion of quality within a democratic society lies beyond the scope set for this book. Our direct concern here must remain with the urgent problems and postponed programmes which are awaiting action from a new and vigorous national leadership. One of the most challenging of all is the future of American farming.

Farm Problems

The most baffling aspect of the agricultural problem is that it is rooted in what almost every other nation would hail as a national blessing : the extraordinary scientific revolution that has been quietly taking place on Americans farms since 1940.

During World War II, we increased agricultural production by thirty per cent, despite the fact that three million of our ablest young farmers were in the armed services. Improved farm machinery, insecticides, fertilizers, new strains of seeds and new planting techniques made all this possible.

The postwar expansion of farm production has continued at an even more explosive rate. In the last ten years output per acre is up eighty-four per cent. In the next decade it can double again.

Yet the total bankruptcy of the present farm programme is illustrated by the fact that since 1953 farm income has sharply decreased, farm surpluses have soared to nearly nine billion dollars' worth, and the annual storage, interest and transportation cost is estimated at one billion dollars. Ezra Taft Benson has spent more money than all the previous secretaries of agriculture in the ninety-seven-year history of the department put together.

The problem of the new Administration in dealing with our agricultural dilemma in 1960 will be complicated by the fact that most farm experts, as well as the leaders of farm organizations, have widely differing views on how it can be resolved.

Indeed, the very complexity of the problem has seemed to disarm the collective national will for a decisive all-out attack on it. Thus we have gone along from year to year with virtually no action at all.

But we cannot continue to abdicate our governmental responsibilities indefinitely. Nor can workable farm programmes be allowed to bog down between obstinate officials in the Department of Agriculture and indignant Congressmen on Capitol Hill responding to localized interests back home.

Yet everyone who seeks to approach our agricultural dilemma in fresh and affirmative terms finds that the entire question is surrounded with social, cultural and even moral sub-questions which are even more difficult than the economic considerations.

What kind of a farm society is best for democratic America? Must we accept the inevitability of giant monopolistic food corporations? Has the family farm no future role to play in the land which gave birth to the most creative democratic development of all time, the Homestead Act?

With these questions in mind, let us briefly outline four specific but closely related courses of action.

First, we should raise our sights much higher on food consumption needs both at home and abroad. Here at home, two-thirds of our children are not now included in the school lunch programme. Moreover, six million American families do not now have a balanced diet.

The need for American food abroad is even more insatiable.

Although the problem of how to get it to those who need it is mechanically difficult, it is not insolvable.

Only a relatively few nations are now able to produce enough food for their people. Stalin's failure in dealing with agricultural problems very nearly caused the collapse of the Soviet regime in the 1930's. The Chinese Communists face an even greater challenge as they seek to feed their soaring population with only 1·7 acres of cultivated land per rural family.

If Communist nations had a capacity equal to ours, they would announce the fact joyously to the whole world and proceed to use their extra production as an instrument of Communist power and diplomacy.

The new Administration which takes over in January 1961 should use our food surpluses not as a lever through which to subvert or buy the loyalty of others, but as instruments of peace and human decency. Here, as elsewhere, moral considerations coincide with the simple arithmetic of our own self-interest.

That is why the Food for Peace programme devised and championed by Senator Hubert Humphrey and others in Congress makes solid good sense.

It includes expanded programmes for grants of surplus commodities for famine and emergency requirements at home and abroad, for needy persons, charitable institutions, and non-profit volunteer agencies; expanded long-term sales of surplus commodities for local currencies abroad; negotiation of agreements for national food reserves; and wider utilization of the foreign currencies accumulated under the present programme.

I should like to see us go further and transport up to one-half of our surplus grain overseas to 'food banks' located in areas in which people are living close to the hunger line.

The savings to American taxpayers each year in storage costs could be as high as $400 million. The storage bins abroad could be built in the recipient nations with local currencies we already own.

We would then undertake to keep these 'food banks' full, to be drawn upon in the case of crop failures, food scarcity leading to inflation, and chronic cases of malnutrition.

Our second goal should be to gear our production and our pricing to meet the requirements of our expanding population and the undernourished millions overseas. This calls for findings of fact about the acreage that will be required to produce for these higher levels of consumption. It also calls for an assurance to our farmers of incomes which reflect the major role they are asked to play in creating an abundant America in a world of lessening tensions.

The most fundamental differences among experts and among working farmers will concern this latter point. Some experts believe that we should simply adjust our present parity and soil bank programmes to production quotas instead of to acreage planted in order to ease the impact of improved technology. Others insist that the answer lies in direct income payments to farmers along the lines of the programme that has worked so well among the wool growers.

Still others assert that a combination of such techniques will be most effective.

But one point is clear : although a problem of this complexity will not yield easily to even the most enlightened and best intentioned experts, further drift must be ruled out. The present pricing programme is intolerable.

A third consideration is the rapid growth of factory-farming systems which stretch from the supermarket chain store direct to the farm and which include processing and marketing as well as production itself. If the day comes when American agriculture is dominated by a few hundred such integrated combinations, our whole democratic society will have been gravely weakened.

Two approaches seem indicated : a system of monopoly restraints on the more destructive speculative elements and the encouragement of marketing co-operatives owned by the farmers themselves. Such co-operatives will require ample low-interest financing and expert management advice.

A fourth and final element in our farm dilemma has received far too little attention and understanding. I refer to the two million farm families which have been forced out of farming by economic pressures in the last seven years. Our national government has made almost no effort to assist their resettlement and to ease their transition into industry.

It is unworthy of our democratic society to stand by with indifference as a major segment of our people see their traditional family livelihood dry up, often with no alternative but to seek a fresh start in a strange environment hundreds or even thousands of miles away.

In the interest of our country's social stability, an orderly, voluntary transition from agriculture to industry should be provided as close to home base as possible.

This means that businesses and communities in the marginal rural areas should be offered low-interest loans, technical assistance, and other inducements to create new sources of employment for displaced farmers in small local plants. It also means that wherever practical, federal expenditures such as defence should be deliberately channelled to plants in these same areas as a matter of public policy.

In suggesting these four objectives, I do not exclude other lines of action. The problem is infinitely complex and there are no easy answers.

Yet for all its vastness, our farm problem is not bigger than the one the nation faced in the Great Depression, when sixteen million men were walking the streets in search of jobs. Despondent and hungry, they passed stores full of food that was spoiling for want of customers.

For three years we said that this intolerable situation was due to 'economic laws' that we had no power to change. But then one day we mustered the nerve to say that it was *we* who made the economic laws and it was we who could change them.

City Problems

According to the *New York Times,* one million New Yorkers now live under slum conditions. In spite of all the efforts made, the number of slum dwellers living there in 1959 was greater than in 1950.

If present trends are allowed to continue, one out of every seven Americans will be living in city slums by 1975.

Yet the problem of our cities, like the problem of our farms, has a positive side which we must recognize. Their very existence reflects the dynamism and vitality of our country, the ceaseless drive of our people to get ahead in the world.

This desire for new opportunities is dramatized by the thirty million Americans who change their residence every year, most of them moving to or within the metropolitan areas. Our traditional restlessness makes our task of urban planning on the necessary scale particularly difficult.

We still want and need the indispensable initiative of individuals and private enterprise in building and rebuilding our central cities and their satellites of suburbs. Yet many areas of action are beyond the means and competence of private individuals alone to undertake, no matter how well financed and intentioned they may be.

In these areas, the power of government – federal, state and local – must be brought into play and closely co-ordinated with private enterprise. Successful examples of this can be found in some four hundred cities in forty-four states and territories where urban renewal projects are under way.

Although the expansion of these programmes will be costly, the stakes are high and we must get on with the task. The cost, moreover, will be spread over many years.

If municipalities are to be encouraged to make comprehensive and practical plans, all sources of income and capital must be budgeted on a three- to five-year basis. This means long-range assurances from both federal and state governments.

Anything less than a comprehensive plan will prove inadequate and wasteful. For instance, there is usually the need to rebuild urban transportation systems as well as to co-ordinate carefully the highway systems which reach into urban centres and vitally affect their future development.

There is the need for more parks, playgrounds and cultural centres; for more and better schools, and for more and better hospitals.

The health of city people is a particularly vital question, especially the municipal problem of air pollution. We must discover safe standards for hydrocarbon concentrations and make every effort to cut down the discharge of contaminants into the air.

The financing problems involved in urban growth are made doubly difficult by the decline or levelling off of the tax base which accompanies the blight that spreads through our cities. Arbitrary, outmoded political and administrative boundaries and unresponsive state governments often discourage decisive community action. Where metropolitan areas cut across state boundaries, these problems are magnified.

Yet precisely because they are big problems, they invite a fresh political inventiveness and leadership.

Housing

The housing programmes we need are related to urban renewal programmes but are also separate from them.

They are separate not only because millions of Americans who want and need new homes do not live in cities, but also because the mere clearing of slums does not build homes for the slum dwellers.

Where shall the slum dwellers, displaced by the rebuilding of dilapidated city areas and their development as business or industrial sites, find a place to live? Uprooted from their own haunts, the displaced slum families wander from temporary lodgings to makeshift lodgings, without knowing where or how to take root. And society pays the price through increasing juvenile delinquency, disease and crime.

When we look beyond this specialized question of slum removal, we see the housing problem in even more dramatic perspective. The notion that there are more homes on the market than there are people to live in them is one hundred and eighty degrees off course.

On the contrary, we need close to one million new homes a year just to take care of our exploding population. We need 300,000 more each year to make up the deficit of homes which are burned, or bulldozed away to make way for new highways, or cleared for urban renewal, or otherwise lost to the housing inventory.

A rate of 1,300,000 new homes a year is thus required to enable us to hold our own. If we are to make any marked dent in our existing *backlog* of thirteen million substandard homes, our building rate must run around two million homes a year. We have been running from one million units to 600,000 units below this requirement annually.

This problem calls for comprehensive and bolder approaches to home-building in cities, suburbs and rural areas. The answers include lowered interest rates, lower down payments, the modification of building techniques to take advantage of new low-cost methods of construction, and an end to artificial obstacles such as feather-bedding and outmoded local building codes.

This calls for a co-ordinated and greatly expanded attack on our building requirements in which business, government and labour work closely together. With our sights high, and with the knowledge that the government will use its power over credit to maintain the necessary purchasing power, we can begin to put these restrictive practices behind us.

A massive increase in new home-building will strengthen the social fabric of American life. And as usual, everyone also stands to gain in the most *material* way if the right things are done with the public good in mind.

Education

In an earlier chapter we examined the dramatically creative role American education has played in the unfolding development of our American society. But in today's world, the challenge is taking on even broader implications.

On the one hand, we are faced with a fast-rising birth-rate, a disturbing shortage of well-qualified teachers, and increasingly inadequate schools.

On the other hand is the growing realization that the quality of our education must be substantially improved if the new generation is to cope effectively with the infinitely complex new world into which we are moving.

At present, we are spending about three per cent of our gross national income on the education of the forty-six million boys and girls now attending school and college. Yet we urgently need 140,000 more classrooms and 135,000 more teachers.

The rapid increase in the birth-rate will further increase the pressure on our educational system, and particularly on our universities, in the coming years.

Some of the load will continue to be borne by private and parochial educational institutions. Most of these, however, are presently caught in the financial dilemma of limited endowments side by side with soaring costs.

Federal income-tax credits up to certain amounts on tuitions paid by parents or sponsors of students in private institutions could be one form of appropriate federal investment in the education of our next generation.

Traditionally the major cost of our public school systems has been paid for by the communities themselves, with funds largely raised from taxes on real estate. In recent years the states have assumed more of the load.

Now it has become clear that state and local revenues cannot meet the need. Federal funds without federal interference are the only alternative if we are not to repudiate our national promise of good education for every child as the basis for equal opportunities for all Americans.

Medical Care

One of the most exciting areas for economic and human development is in the field of health and medicine. We have never begrudged the spending of billions of dollars to defend ourselves from Communist attack. But we have lagged in providing the needed dollars to assure long, happy and productive lives through medical research.

Although we still have far to go, medical research has produced magnificent results in recent years. Investments in basic research have already led to dramatic discoveries such as the Salk polio vaccine, the tranquillizing drugs and physical energizers that have been used with such success in the treatment of mental illness, and the anti-coagulants that have brought so much help to those afflicted with heart disease and strokes.

Our doctors and scientists are also working modern miracles in the development of hormone compounds for the treatment of arthritis, blinding eye diseases, skin diseases and allergic conditions. The National Institute of Arthritis and Metabolic diseases reports a new pain-killing drug, NIH-7519, ten times more potent than morphine and apparently less addictive.

Best of all, every dollar that we have invested in medical research has paid off in longer lives free of illness and pain. Even the most fervent opponents of the Welfare State will be impressed by the fact that the number of people saved from death by government-supported medical research have already paid three times as much in taxes as the cost of the research which saved them.

But much remains to be done. Tens of thousands still die each year of cancer.

Nearly sixteen million Americans are disabled by diseases of the heart and circulation, including cerebral vascular diseases.

Nearly eleven million Americans are disabled by arthritis and rheumatic diseases.

If we fail to bend every effort to cure these crippling

diseases, we not only condone human misery; we waste our greatest natural resource, which is the individual vitality, labour and inventiveness of the people of the United States.

To provide the funds and organization for effective national defence against disease, the federal government should provide a clearing house for the organization of experiments done in research centres and universities throughout the country. In addition, the government should increase its own participation in research by expanding the work done by such organizations as the National Institutes of Health, including the National Institute of Mental Health and the National Heart Institute.

The field of health is filled with limitless challenges. There can be no better way to show our belief in the brotherhood of man than by waging sustained war on disease with the peaceful weapons of scientific research and making the results available to people everywhere.

Surely there is no more realistic way to volunteer in the Party of Hope.

Natural Resources

It is now over fifty years since President Theodore Roosevelt called the conservation of natural resources a primary challenge to America. 'Unless we solve that problem,' he proclaimed on October 4th, 1907, 'it will avail us little to solve all others. To solve it, the whole Nation must undertake the task.'

A few months later he told the nation's forty-four Governors assembled at the first White House Conference on Conservation :

Disregarding for the moment the question of moral purpose, it is safe to say that the prosperity of our people depends directly on the energy and intelligence with which our natural resources are used.

It is ominously evident that these resources are in the course of rapid exhaustion. In the past we have admitted the right of the individual to injure the future of the Republic for his own present profit.

As a people we have the right and the duty to protect ourselves and our children against the wasteful development of our natural resources, whether that waste is caused by the actual destruction of such resources or by making them impossible of development thereafter.

Is there any doubt where Theodore Roosevelt in recent years would have stood in the great but losing struggle in Congress over the Hell's Canyon Dam? Is there any doubt of the scorn and contempt he would have had for those who identified the preservation of our nation's greatest remaining dam site with socialism and budget-busting?

Today, for the shallowest of political and private commercial reasons, only a portion of the vast hydroelectric energy that would have been available from this great mile-deep chasm will ever be tapped. The series of small private dams now being constructed in place of the high dam at Hell's Canyon will stand as a clear commentary on the timidity and small-mindedness of American leadership at mid-century.

Of course the pressure to exploit has always been stronger and better organized than the incentive or desire to conserve. America's very abundance of timber, water, fertile soil, diverse minerals, fish, plants and animal life has always given us special temptations to despoil our heritage. Few nations have depleted their store of natural resources as rapidly and recklessly as we have.

As Senator Richard Neuberger said not long ago : 'The gutted forests of the lake states, a dozen silty dust bowls, half a thousand polluted rivers, the vanished passenger pigeon and the slaughtered bison of the plains, migratory fish runs choked off from their spawning grounds by chemical wastes and unscreened irrigation ditches, all bear tragic witness to our failure in stewardship.'

Forest preservation through appropriate restrictions on timber operators and enforced retention of seed trees have been common practices in Europe for generations over both private and public users alike.

How long must we wait for the public interest to assert itself squarely and effectively in a national programme against destructive timber-cutting practices?

In addition, we face the danger of a major shortage in our water resources. Already the industrial demand is outrunning our supply in some areas and thus is placing a limit on growth. It requires 300,000 gallons of water, for example, to manufacture one ton of rayon, and the rayon industry in the United States turns out 600,000 tons of rayon a year.

What we must now do – in a way that co-ordinates the powers of the federal, state and local government – is of the following order of magnitude :

We must tap new water sources, and provide for the more efficient use and re-use of existing water resources.

We must develop policies at all levels of government to protect our seashores and river valleys from human exploitation and natural erosion.

We must recognize that the recreational use of water, and our other natural resources, is often as important a public use as the production of goods and merchandise.

We must make an all-out attack on water pollution.

We must perfect present techniques for cutting down water losses through evaporation.

We should encourage further experiments in the purifying of sea water for its use at low, commercial prices.

We need more irrigation and land reclamation progress, more dams and flood-control projects.

Above all, we must develop institutions which can handle land and water problems on a regional basis, corresponding not to artificial political boundaries but to the special aspects of the region's watershed and water resources situation.

In all that we do in the natural resource field, we can never have a better guide than the objectives framed by Gifford Pinchot, Republican Governor of Pennsylvania, and America's first great conservationist: 'The rightful use and purpose of our natural resources is to make all the people strong and well, able and wise, well taught, well fed, well clothed, well housed, full of knowledge and initiative, with equal opportunity for all and special privilege for none.'

Social Welfare

Social insurance is one of the great levers that has raised the assurance of minimum living standards so spectacularly in the past generation. Yet much as we may applaud the concept of our social insurance plans, the fact remains that a great number of improvements are needed in the structure of existing plans if they are to be kept relevant to our needs.

This means that we must constantly reconsider the adequacy of our unemployment compensation programme, our programmes for workmen's compensation, for disability income, and for medical care.

There is one programme in particular which has been too long minimized and which I feel should engage our sympathies and our energies to the hilt. This is the need for improved efforts to care for our elderly people.

Thanks to our advances in the biological sciences, we may all expect to live longer. This expectation itself creates a set of economic and emotional problems which former generations of Americans did not bother about. They are real problems, and they demand a thoughtful and humane solution.

For one thing, we should examine our practice of providing automatic cut-off age dates for active productive work, regardless of whether or not the individual likes his work, wants to continue at it, and is fully capable of good performance.

To most Americans, the work we do becomes as much a part of us as the very air we breathe. It is the source of our self-respect, of personal usefulness, the feeling that we are part of the flow of life.

Nothing can prove more demoralizing to a vigorous man or woman who wants to work than to be told that he will no longer be encouraged or even allowed to do so because of employment practices in private firms or because of federal and state regulations.

America is rich in human resources; but not so rich that our communities can afford to dispense with the services of men and women of proved capacity and experience who are capable of working past the usual retirement age of sixty-five.

These men and women should be encouraged to remain active and contributing members of their communities as long as they are physically able to do so and wish to do so.

This does not mean that those who wish to retire at sixty-five should be put at a disadvantage in the operations of our Social Security laws. They are entitled to relax free of want in their later years.

Retirement, however, is not easy under our present programmes. The purchasing power of Social Security benefits has been reduced by inflation, and in many cases is now hopelessly inadequate. Benefits should be adjusted as in several other countries, to wipe out this disadvantage.

Another factor is housing. It is difficult for most American families to provide adequate housing under their own roof for an elderly father, mother or both. Thus the latter come to feel that they are an unwanted extra burden. At best, living with an elderly parent or parents in the household, with all the complicated sensitivities involved, leads to tensions.

The answer to this problem, made more acute by modern urban living, lies in low-cost, specially designed housing for elderly people, where they can continue to be happy with friends and family nearby and with medical care and other social services available to keep them in good health and spirits.

Private enterprise, once it puts its ingenuity to work on this human need, can do much to meet it. Our federal, state and local governments have their own special obligations.

Transportation

Our transportation network helps determine the manner and rate at which most communities grow and prosper. It often spells the difference between boom towns and ghost towns. In times of war, it can determine our capacity for survival.

Yet almost every study reveals that our present transportation system is inadequate and steadily becoming more so.

In the East many of our railroads are barely breaking even, while their equipment grows more obsolete and their service less efficient. It would be scandalous to allow this disintegration to continue.

If direct government subsidies are required to keep railroads serving cities whose future prosperity requires their services, let us face the facts and provide those subsidies, as our grandfathers were so ready to do and which every nation on earth except America does today.

The movement of freight by truck and passenger traffic by bus and private auto also grows steadily and unsurely. And with that increase we find ourselves confronted with the need for more and more new highways with better wearing surfaces and more lanes to carry heavy traffic.

Airport facilities are also increasingly jammed up. For the want of adequate runways on the ground, the danger of air collision between aircraft overhead waiting for a landing signal grows steadily more acute. The heavy increase in the use of jet aircraft will compound this problem enormously.

Although each field of transportation has its special problems, we need an overall national transportation policy designed to serve the best interests of industry and the public by a more rational use of all of our various modes of transportation, each modernized and adequate. And we need it soon.

This is only a partial catalogue of the tasks awaiting our attention in the 1960's if we are to extend our frontiers of economic abundance and give new meaning to the American Dream.

This list of national needs is long enough, however, to suggest that we have by no means mastered our economic problems or reached the end of our strivings for a better life. No generation of Americans can rest on the work of its predecessors. Indeed, the work that remains to be done exceeds all we have done in the past.

The needs which I have sketched have been gradually accumulating. In recent years our slow pace of economic growth has added greatly to the backlog. It cannot be wiped out overnight.

Although the cost of action now that the problems are full blown is far greater than the cost of timely action earlier would have been, the Administration elected in 1960 must vigorously get ahead with the job.

We have seen that our productive capacity can be greatly expanded, although there are limits even to that. Correction of our present restrictive monetary policies alone would enable the new Administration to make a generous down payment on the cost of these economic programmes. Indeed, our whole additional effort for 1961 could be paid for from funds we might now be saving if we could reduce present interest rates to former levels.

Yet this remains a programme not for a year but for a decade. The essential thing is that we raise our sights to the overall requirements, and confidently get on with the task of building a stronger and ever more abundant America.

May I add that our *pursuit* of abundance must be more than a mere national striving for security and comfort. Our objective is new dignity for each individual citizen, in a community that provides deepening satisfactions, in a world at peace.

PART IV

The Politics of Peace

Freedom is an indivisible word. If we want to enjoy it we must be prepared to extend it to all peoples, whether they be rich or poor, whether they agree with us or not, no matter what their race or the colour of their skin.

WENDELL WILLKIE

One World, 1944

CHAPTER XVI

The Situation in Perspective

WE NOW come to a crucial point. As a practical matter, is the promise and capacity of America really relevant to today's world?

Can we effectively reshape our traditional sense of purpose, our dedication to individual rights, and our economic resources to give them new strength when everywhere else old ways are being overthrown and old values challenged?

As we seek answers to this question, we come face to face with some bewildering uncertainties. Since the Korean War, for example, we have spent $250 billion to develop what we assumed to be an impenetrable defence system. Yet most military experts now sharply question its adequacy.

We have spent more billions to help less fortunate people help themselves. Yet American prestige in most parts of the world has been at a low ebb, and many of those whom we eagerly seek as friends question our judgment and even our motives.

When we turn to our leaders for assurance, they tell us that there is no relief in sight. They assert that proposals for more than token disarmament are illusory. They admit the possibility that a single miscalculation in Moscow, Peking, Washington or elsewhere could in a matter of hours leave our cities a shambles and more than half of us dead.

When we ask what the answer is they tell us that there is no alternative but to learn to live indefinitely with terror.

For a people who have never known physical fear in their 185-year history, this is a new and shattering prospect. Thus far, to be sure, it stands to the credit of the American character that we have not only refused to panic, but that we have searched in a calm and realistic manner for a way out of the darkness.

I like to think that when the spirit of American democracy is most effective, it is most akin to the spirit of prophecy in its vigorous Judaeo-Christian form.

Such prophecy immerses itself deeply in the immediate situation. It seeks the stern alternatives of the age, and defines what they are. It brings the individual electrifyingly close to those alternatives. It tells him that if one alternative is embraced as a guide for action, the result will be this; while if it is rejected, the result will be that.

Nowhere does it say that the future, for good or ill, has already been sealed and placed out of reach beyond further alteration.

Instead it proclaims that if the alternatives are bravely confronted, if enough of the best of human reason and will-power are brought to bear on them, there may be a fresh beginning.

If ever this spirit of prophecy was needed, it is needed now.

The new leadership which will assume national responsibility in January 1961, must deal with the full force of the three simultaneous revolutions to which I alluded in an earlier chapter.

The first is the revolution of rising expectations. Some billion and a half people in Asia, Africa and Latin America are struggling not only for political independence, but to remove the blight of poverty, disease, illiteracy and static despair; to erase the memory of racial subservience; to stand in the sun with their own distinctive personality; to be recognized for their own human worth.

Second, there is the industrial and technological revolution of the Soviet Union, augmented and complicated recently by the spectacular rise of Communist China.

Third, there is the revolution in armament and weapons systems, which now confronts the world with the very real possibility of atomic destruction.

Taken one by one, these three revolutions would constitute an unprecedented challenge to the American people. Each divorced from all the rest would in its own way call for a profound change in our traditional responses to world events.

But by superimposing all three revolutions one on top of the other, history has granted them free rein to multiply their mutually explosive power.

This fact has not been lost on the Communists. Both their policy statements and their actions reflect their keen awareness of the interplay.

The total challenge is unique, and inevitably we Americans feel frustrated by its implications. This leads us to minimize our accomplishments since 1945, while maximizing those of the Soviet Union.

Let us start therefore by listing some of our successes side by side with Soviet failures. This will help improve our perspective by demonstrating that our performance in a series of totally new situations has been remarkably creative, while in many respects that of the Kremlin has been less successful than is generally assumed.

Since 1945 we can list the following positive accomplishments :

First was our generous and constructive treatment of our late enemies, Germany and Japan.

On the physical front, we poured out billions of dollars to restore their shattered economies and cities. On the political front, we moved to bring them back to full membership in the community of free nations.

Second, although we alone had the atomic bomb and the means of delivering it, we offered to place atomic weapons and atomic energy under international control. And we did this not from timidity, but from a deeply felt national sense of responsibility for the preservation of the civilization which nurtured us all.

Third, we did not try to coerce other nations into joining an American empire in order to offset the strength of the Communist tyranny with its roots in the Soviet empire.

Instead, without attaching any political strings, we offered aid to those nations who wanted to help themselves attain and preserve the conditions for genuine national freedom and independence.

The first steps came in 1946 with the British Loan, the checking of Soviet penetration of Iran, and our support of Turkey against Soviet attempts to gain a foothold in the Dardanelles.

Then came the Truman Doctrine to bolster Greece and Turkey, which represented an extraordinarily bold break with our isolationist past.

'I believe,' said President Truman on March 12th, 1947, 'that it must be the policy of the United States to support free peoples who are resisting attempted subjugation by armed minorities or by outside pressures.'

'The President's message faces the facts,' said Republican Senator Vandenberg, of Michigan, 'and so must the Congress.' And so it did.

Fourth, came the Marshall Plan. In May 1947, Sir Winston Churchill referred to Western and Central Europe as a 'rubble heap, a charnel house, a breeding ground of pestilence and hate'.

A month later at Harvard, Secretary of State Marshall observed that unless we provided prompt massive economic assistance Europe would face 'economic, social and political deterioration of a very grave character'.

The assistance programme which General Marshall proposed was not directed against any country, but only against 'hunger, poverty, desperation, and chaos'. Its purpose 'should be the revival of a working economy in the world so as to permit the emergence of political and social conditions in which free institutions can exist'.

We did not call upon the recipients of American aid to join us in a military alliance; we asked only that they work and co-operate with us as partners in a great humanitarian enterprise.

There was a wideness in Marshall's vision that far transcended the exercise of American power for the sake of power itself. His appeal was to a common interest in independence, in the restoration of Europe's self-respect and confidence in itself, in widening its freedom of choice.

The London *Economist* spoke for most people in Western Europe when it described the Marshall Plan aid as 'the most straightforwardly generous thing that any country has ever done for others, the fullest expression so far of that American idealism on which all the hopes of the West depend'.

The fact that it was enlightened generosity which served our own long-term national interests takes nothing away from the intrinsic value of the deed.

Fifth, came the Berlin airlift, our answer in 1948 to the Soviet blockade of all land traffic routes between Berlin and the West.

The Allied response to this challenge, inspired and organized by America, was sharp, bold, unequivocal and successful.

Sixth, came technical and economic assistance for underdeveloped nations.

In his Inaugural Address in January 1949, President Truman expanded this concept of creative economic and political action beyond Europe through his 'Point Four' proposal. 'We must embark on a bold new programme,' he said, 'for making the benefits of our scientific advances and industrial progress available for the improvement and growth of underdeveloped areas.'

The technical assistance contemplated under the Point Four programme was later supplemented by direct grants of financial help. The plan was conceived as a world-wide, continuing programme of helping underdeveloped nations to help themselves in a battle against their ancient enemies – hunger, misery and despair.

'It recognized the historic fact,' said President Truman in his memoirs, 'that colonialism had run its course and could no longer be made to work for a few favoured nations.'

Through such positive efforts we began to see that the

industrially advanced nations of the West could offer the underdeveloped nations not only the ideal of political democracy, but the material assistance to help them create societies in which poverty could gradually be eased and the basis for a massive expansion through their own will and resources established.

Seventh, was the launching in April 1949 of the North Atlantic Treaty Organization, representing the first peacetime military alliance concluded by the United States since the adoption of the Constitution.

It was born of a clearly recognized need to provide concrete reassurance to our European friends who were beset with a nagging fear that their continent would be overrun by the Soviet Army before effective help could arrive. Only an inclusive security system could dispel these fears.

Historical experience had indicated that a common military command between allies could only be achieved after war had broken out, and sometimes with difficulty even then.

In form and purpose, therefore, NATO was altogether new under the sun. It called for a welding together of the national armies of Europe and North America into a common defence system with a common command and a common plan – in order to prevent war from occurring in the first place. The Soviet Union was put on notice that its attack on any member of NATO would be considered an attack on all.

Eighth was our subsequent response to the first case of overt Communist aggression – the invasion of South Korea by North Korean forces in June 1950.

President Truman has left us an account of what went through his mind when the news of this attack brought him flying back to Washington from his home in Independence, Missouri.

I had time to think aboard the plane [he has written]. In my generation, this was not the first occasion when the strong had attacked the weak. I recalled some earlier instances: Manchuria, Ethiopia, Austria. I remembered how each time that the democracies failed to act it had encouraged the aggressors to keep going ahead.

If the Communists were permitted to force their way into the Republic of Korea without opposition from the free world, no small nation would have the courage to resist threats and aggressions by stronger Communist neighbours. This could lead to a third world war, just as similar incidents had brought on the Second World War.

It was also clear that the foundations and the principles of the United Nations were at stake unless this unprovoked attack on Korea could be stopped.

Although embittering political differences later developed on the conduct and objectives of the war, the initial unity of the American people behind this great decision was extraordinary. Its effects in deterring further aggression were certainly far-reaching.

Thus we see that in a period of global crisis calling for action without precedent in our history, American policy makers performed boldly and creatively. Equally important, the American people without regard to political lines shook off their isolationist habits of mind to give them overwhelming support.

To place this chronicle of positive and effective action in still clearer perspective, let us list briefly some of the areas where Soviet policy during this same period proved a failure.

1. The Soviet Union, as the foe of a united Europe, failed to fill the expected postwar vacuum between the Oder-Neisse River and the British Channel.

2. The Soviets failed in their efforts to build an effective world ideology based on the concepts of Lenin and the Russian Revolution.

The Kremlin's continued insistence on treating other Communist parties and governments as mere adjuncts of the Soviet

Union weakened the world movement. The disenchantment of Tito and the Yugoslavs brought this fact home to the world.

3. The Soviets failed in their effort to incorporate Eastern Europe successfully into their political system.

For fourteen years, Soviet-dominated regimes have been imposed on East Germany, Poland, Hungary, Czechoslovakia, Bulgaria, Rumania and Albania. They have had a clear field for Soviet propaganda, indoctrination, economic organization and purges.

Yet events in Budapest and Warsaw in 1956 made it clear that the peoples of these nations now share one primary wish : to cut the political and economic bonds that tie them to the Kremlin and to develop in their own way.

4. The Soviets have failed to win over the new Asian nations either by intimidation or subversion. In each case except one, the 1948 Communist uprisings which were launched almost simultaneously throughout Asia fizzled out. Only in French Indochina, and in that case largely because of French and American miscalculations, was it even partially successful.

5. The Soviets have failed in their campaign to turn the Soviet people against the Atlantic Community and particularly against the Americans.

Everyone who visits the Soviet Union senses an enormous goodwill toward Americans. I can testify personally that the individual Russians one meets in offices, factories, schools, universities, farms and on trains, want nothing so much as understanding and friendship with America.

6. The Soviets have even failed to turn their own young people into blind followers of Communist doctrine. After two generations of total Soviet education, it was assumed that the 'new Socialist man' would accept the philosophic basis of socialism without question and be impervious to 'capitalist' habits. Yet this has not yet occurred.

To be sure, the Soviet series of five-year plans have been massive and, by and large, successful efforts to create the capital needed for rapid industrial expansion. The Russian people have been persuaded and pressured into labouring hard and asking little in return.

But the peasants, the workers and the minor bureaucrats on whom the major workaday burden falls are no longer satisfied with the promise of a glorious Socialist future for generations yet unborn. They want a fairer return on their labour in terms of improving living standards, and they want it now.

CHAPTER XVII

Communist Objectives and Strategy

THIS brief review shows a reassuring number of American successes and Soviet failures during the postwar period. Even more important, it indicates what America is capable of doing under affirmative, sensitive leadership.

Yet a close look at the long-range prospects as they have been developing since the Korean stalemate provides no basis for complacency. If a new leadership in January 1961 is to deal effectively with the far less advantageous situation now shaping up, it must look the hard facts straight in the face, and then come up with some fresh approaches.

Before we consider the new requirements, however, it may be helpful to consider as precisely as we can what the Soviet Union is striving to accomplish.

There is every evidence that the Kremlin still assumes the validity of Lenin's belief that Communism is destined to dominate the world.

By all odds the most powerful force that stands in the way of Soviet ambitions is the 500 million highly skilled and industrialized people who live in Western Europe and North America.

The Kremlin's primary tactic, therefore, must be to split this counterforce at the natural dividing line – the Atlantic Ocean.

If Western Europe's vast production could be combined directly or indirectly with that of the Soviet Union, the aggregate would exceed that of the United States. The United States could then be isolated and forced to choose between a war it could not win or the acceptance of Communist direction of world affairs.

Given the clear Soviet objective of dividing Western Europe from America, the object has been pursued by two different but related tactics.

The first called for direct pressure – industrial, economic, political and military – against our NATO allies in Europe. This was the best-known feature of Stalinism after World War II, and we met it successfully.

The second way called for a flanking attack through the churning continents of Asia, Africa and Latin America, which contain the raw materials on which Europe's prosperity depends and where revolutionary change is the order of the day.

If the Soviets could secure a grip on a reasonable fraction of these raw materials it could present an appealing political case to many uncertain Western European leaders, backed if necessary by ruthless economic pressures.

'Now we can supply your needs,' the Kremlin might say, 'at substantially lower prices. We do not ask you to change your form of government. Simply pull out of NATO. Stop taking directions from those trigger-happy Americans. Bind your economic future more closely to the unlimited resources and markets of the Soviet Union and China. We, not America, represent the future.'

The concept behind this second tactic goes back to Lenin's statement forty years ago that 'the road to Paris lies through Calcutta and Peking'. Five years later, Stalin echoed him. 'The backs of the British' [meaning the West], he said, 'will be broken not on the river Thames, but on the Yangtze, the Ganges, and the Nile.'

Both men believed that International Communism could win command over a heavily industrialized Europe by establishing its control over a sizable fraction of the resources of Asia and Africa.

Fortunately, Stalin lacked the capital, the technicians and the understanding of peasant Asia to follow this approach effectively. But Khrushchev has the resources and the political astuteness that Stalin lacked. He is now using them both with vigour and skill.

This development was clearly foreseeable long before American policies made any adjustments to meet it. In 1953, for instance, I discussed its possibilities at length in my book, *Ambassador's Report*.

Our government, however, continued to scoff at such Soviet capabilities until Sputnik and the repeated warnings of men like Mr Allen Dulles, Director of our Central Intelligence Agency, finally convinced it that a distasteful political system is not necessarily an unworkable one.

In the meantime our military strategy and that of our NATO allies have been rendered increasingly obsolete.

In 1949 the United States had a decisive superiority in atomic weapons and the means of delivering them. Russia relied solely on its huge conventional ground forces.

The original strategic conception of NATO was effectively tailored to fit this situation. It assumed that a small but respectable Anglo-American-European ground and air force would be enough to deter or slow down any surprise Soviet invasion of Western Europe aided by Communist uprisings.

A major invasion, requiring the full mobilization of Soviet strength, would be deterred or broken up by the nuclear armed bombers of the United States Strategic Air Command and the British Royal Air Force.

This assumption is no longer valid.

The NATO ground forces which were originally planned have not been developed. Some British and most French forces have been withdrawn from Europe. The German contingent, slow in developing, is now equal to the British, larger than the French, and soon will furnish more than half of all the forces in NATO's key central army. Yet Germany's role in World War II still lingers menacingly in the memory of many Europeans.

The net result is a NATO force that is inadequate in a military sense and politically and psychologically unbalanced.

Meanwhile, there has been a radical shift in the balance of strategic *nuclear* power. Russia has broken the American monopoly on atomic and hydrogen weapons and on the means for delivering them. Indeed by 1963 the nuclear striking power of the Soviet Union, based on its faster missile development, may be superior to our own.

Military experts are concerned that this superiority, coupled with the comparative lack of progress we are making defensively, may tempt the Kremlin to destroy United States retaliatory power by a sudden blow. Soviet intercontinental missiles hitting our cities, and intermediate-range missiles raining down on our air bases, could gravely weaken our capacity to retaliate before many of our planes got off the ground.

Predictions are risky, and there are certainly many powerful non-military factors restraining the Kremlin from initiating a surprise attack of this kind. Nevertheless, as long as this situation exists, it would be dangerous to ignore it in our planning.

If the nuclear power balance should indeed slip toward Moscow, most Asians, many Europeans and a sizable number of Americans may be tempted to adjust to the new reality without waiting for the Kremlin to demonstrate its capacity. Thus the mere *existence* of Soviet military superiority could pave the way for diplomatic victories of the first magnitude.

Other developments of a related character have already

prepared a psychological climate favourable to a Soviet tactic of this kind. One is the fact that Soviet science, best symbolized by Sputnik, has made startling advances. These accomplishments have caught the imagination of the world and profoundly shaken the world's belief in American technical supremacy.

The second fact is our failure to win a clear decision in the Korean War, which punctured the illusions of American military might gained during the defeat of Japan.

In a wholly different dimension of power and diplomacy, Russia has profited from the near total failure of American policy in regard to China.

The failure has stemmed from our inability to grasp the broad inner meaning of what has been happening on the far side of the Pacific. The effect of American policy has been to bring Communist Russia and Communist China into a relationship where each, for its own purposes, can use America as the devil in any piece of business either means to transact.

Thus in the first years following Chiang Kai-shek's retreat to Formosa in 1949, we looked on the new government in Peking as another backward satellite of the Soviet Union. Even after Red China had fought the United Nations forces to a standstill in Korea, we continued to assume that this Asian 'junior partner' of the Kremlin would conveniently collapse.

These illusions led us into inept diplomatic manoeuvres that had little relevance to the facts. The 'unleashings' and 'releashings', the threats of massive retaliation, of naval blockades of the Chinese coast, served only to frighten our friends in Europe and many in South and East Asia as well.

In no way did these gestures arrest the consolidation by the Communist leaders of their power on the Chinese mainland. On the contrary, they served as pretexts for their ever more vigorous consolidation of power. Whipping up hatred against the United States as the arch-enemy of 'Chinese democratic freedom' was easy, cheap and productive.

Recently we have shifted to the opposite extreme. When it seemed apparent that Mao's influence in 1958 had caused Khrushchev to turn away from a summit meeting, some American observers began to say that here was proof positive that the Chinese tail was now able to wag the Soviet dog.

What really goes on between Moscow and Peking is obscure. But two assumptions seem tenable.

First, the balance of influence between the two is probably in flux, with each partner forced in various ways to accommodate itself somewhat to the ambitions and fears of the other.

Second, almost surely Moscow and Peking view our fast-changing world from different perspectives, and approach them from different motivations.

The contrasting attitudes of the U.S.S.R. and China on such matters as the summit meeting, the Eisenhower–Khruschev visits, and the Chinese–Indian border controversy are all recent cases in point.

These differences, which may grow, stem primarily from the fact that the Soviet Union is a nation with almost un-limited natural resources and a population not much bigger than our own, while Red China, with one-fifth the world's population, is pressed into a relatively limited land area with limited natural resources.

The latter situation has an explosive potential, particularly when we remember that the Chinese are a vital people bordered by several weaker nations which offer tempting territory into which to expand.

The expansion of Japan and Hitler's Germany in similar circumstances provides classic examples of this situation. So did the colonial expansion of Spain, Britain, France and Holland in earlier epochs when sea power was a decisive factor in world politics.

The Soviet Union presents a totally different picture. With

its ample natural resources and room for population growth, the historic reasons for aggressive expansion do not appear to exist.

It would be folly, of course, to discount the *ideological* pressures which are inherent in Communism itself. Nevertheless, as Soviet living standards rise with the further rapid development of Soviet industry, the Kremlin would appear to have a diminishing number of reasons to risk war for territorial or economic gains.

The traditional ideological objectives could more safely be served by the internal subversion of key countries by local Communists, and by striving to disarm the will of those countries which oppose the spread of Soviet influence by nuclear blackmail.

China is now seeking to feed its vast population through a brutally regimented system of agricultural communes. At the same time, ambitious plans for rapid industrialization are being pressed vigorously.

The titanic pressure which this effort is bringing to bear on Chinese land and mineral resources could be eased by the comradely sharing of the Soviet eastern lands with Chinese colonizers so that China's rapid industrialization could proceed on schedule. Khrushchev has publicly alluded to such a possibility.

This would bring nearly one-third of the world's population together in an economic, political and military colossus stretching from Berlin to Canton. It is a chilling prospect which may have considerable appeal to whatever may be left of the Stalinist element within the Soviet hierarchy.

But there are some formidable physical, nationalist and human obstacles in the way of its fulfilment. The limitations of climate and water, for example, make Siberian agriculture a season-to-season gamble. Moreover, the physical merging of Soviet and Chinese national and human resources would mean the Kremlin's repudiation of its promise of a better life for the Russian people.

Another barrier is the national pride and security of the Soviet Union itself. Economic and political integration on a scale sufficient to solve China's resource hunger would be a giant step toward Chinese domination of the Soviet Union, the Communist movement and, ultimately, of the world itself. It is unlikely, therefore, that the Kremlin, under present circumstances, will co-operate in such a development.

Alternatively, the Chinese Communist leaders may increasingly seek to solve their economic and political dilemma by pressure toward the south. The land there is fertile, blessed with rich soil, ample rainfall and a warm, year-round sun that assures two or even three crops annually.

Some areas, such as Java, are greatly overpopulated. But nearby Sumatra could absorb thirty to forty million more people. Burma could support far more than its present population. So could the Philippines, South Vietnam, Cambodia, Laos, Thailand and Malaya.

If the Chinese leadership decides further to increase its pressure into these lush lands to the south, they will present both Soviet and American policy makers with a fishhook tangle of dilemmas. India, as a potential counterbalance, would assume a central role, the full importance of which has gradually become more apparent as Chinese–Indian relations have deteriorated.

All this, of course, is still conjecture. So are the implications for America in the event the U.S.S.R. and Communist China are led by their different motivations to follow increasingly divergent lines of action in world politics.

Is it not possible that the force of these conflicts and stirrings may soon press the Kremlin toward a fateful decision: either to take the historic step of tying its economic and political destiny to China at an early stage when it can hope to assume and maintain its dominance; or, as an alternative, to seek a genuine understanding with the Atlantic powers which will enable it to deal more independently with its great and ambitious Asian neighbour?

Although our present national leadership appears very nearly blind to these long-term possibilities, the new Administration that takes office in January 1961 may well be called upon to deal with them. If it is to do so effectively, it will need a sophisticated freshness and imagination in dealing with the evolving challenge of Communism in its new and different shapes and forms.

Some embittered Democrats in particular will need to discard the complexes which they accumulated during the witch-hunting days of the late 1940's and early 1950's.

They know that any Democratic Vice-President who barnstormed the Soviet Union as Vice-President Nixon did would have been labelled 'soft on Communism' by his Republican opponents. They know that any Democratic President who took the initiative in exchanging transoceanic visits with Khrushchev, as President Eisenhower did, would have been called a 'dupe of the Kremlin'.

This creates an understandable temptation to retaliate by militantly attacking any Administration effort to move off dead centre.

Fortunately, only a minority of Democratic leaders have succumbed to this temptation. Most of them know that the Communist challenge is far too dangerous to approach with anything less than objectivity and insight.

CHAPTER XVIII

Asia, Africa and Latin America

ANOTHER area of weakness in American foreign policy involves our failure to devise and sustain a more affirmative approach to the developing continents of Asia, Africa and Latin America, which have a vital and perhaps decisive role to play in the years ahead.

Our policies in these continents still appear to be based on the assumption that the principal threat to their orderly political growth is from overt Soviet–Chinese military aggression.

This possibility cannot, of course, be discounted. In South Vietnam, South Korea and Taiwan the possibility of Communist attack is real. Similar possibilities exist in the Middle East.

But in two whole continents – South America and Africa – and in much of the vast arc of Asia that stretches from Lebanon to Manila, the primary threat to world peace comes not from Soviet tanks and jets but from economic strangulation, injustice and human frustration.

In areas which are not clearly exposed to Communist armed aggression, American military aid programmes, which have often been launched with scant understanding of their economic and political repercussions, seldom coincide with our long-term security interests. Much less do they coincide with the long-term interests of the people in the country concerned.

In instance after instance we have seen those ill-conceived military programmes foster regional tensions, divert internal energies from constructive economic efforts, pave the way for palace revolutions, and tie our prestige and our influence to the dubious tenure of dictators who sooner or later are destined to be swept aside.

There are many ways in which a wobbly new government

may be undermined. But none is more certain than to allow its leaders to embark unnecessarily on an excessive military programme that distracts them from such essential tasks as growing rice, driving out malaria, building schools, clinics and roads, and creating the foundations of a good society.

Our economic efforts have themselves been weakened by lack of realistic standards for the distribution of our assistance. Although all developing nations need help to enable them to become viable, they vary widely in their capacity to use our assistance effectively.

Why is it, for example, that a dam can be built and operated with great success in one Asian country, while in another country a similar dam is a miserable failure?

Why is it that modern equipment in some countries can make a vital contribution to increasing agricultural and industrial productivity, while similar machinery, sent to others, lies rusting on the docks?

The developing countries fall into many categories. At one end, a few, such as India, Pakistan, Philippines, Israel, and Taiwan, possess the leadership, the civil service and the management skills to put long-term investments of American capital to good use. At the opposite end of the scale are those nations which are totally incapable of absorbing major assistance until their economic and administrative structures are in better order.

When we press the latter to march at an economic pace that is beyond their capacity, we face near-certain failure, and when the failure comes it leads to bitterness on their part and frustration on ours.

In rare cases, of course, there are persuasive short-term reasons for providing substantial aid even when we know that it cannot be effectively used. Usually these reasons will be related to special activity on the part of Communist minorities. Yet here, unless we watch our step, we may appear to be offering a premium to those countries which have the most

Communists, thereby turning the local Communist minority into a national resource like uranium or petroleum.

After 1954, this curious premium on Communism actually was written into the preamble of the Mutual Security Act by language that implied that our aid programme would be continued only as long as the Communist danger exists.

This enabled local Communist leaders to suggest that a double debt of gratitude was owed to the Kremlin : first, for the aid it gave to the recipient nations in its own right, and second, for the aid they frightened us Americans into giving. In 1959, I proposed and Congress adopted a new, more affirmative official statement of purpose.

A negative, insensitive approach to foreign economic aid has also led us into other errors. For instance, we have seemed to assume that hungry Asians, Africans and Latin Americans can be turned into orderly supporters of the *status quo* simply by filling their stomachs.

This view reflects a massive misunderstanding of the Communist appeal and, indeed, of human nature. Frustrations which grow from injustice and the lack of a sense of participation in community life and development are far stronger motivations toward Communism than hunger pure and simple.

Indeed, any Asian, African or Latin-American government which assumes that food can be substituted for dignity and justice may end up with a better-nourished and therefore more effective Communist minority than it had in the first place.

The assumption that American aid will enable us to purchase political support for whatever position we choose to take in the United Nations is equally cynical and equally in error.

Such miscalculations reflect the failure of many American leaders in both the State Department and Congress to understand the nature of the revolution for human dignity, freedom and opportunity, and the manner in which this revolution is shaping events in the developing continents.

It may be added that our ability to cope more effectively

with this situation has been gravely handicapped by the ineptitude and inexperience of many Americans who have been sent overseas.

We can no longer afford to distribute ambassadorships or lesser administrative posts as rewards to campaign contributors with little or no knowledge of economics and history and even less of government and politics.

The Ugly American has recently popularized the picture of tremendous numbers of our most boorish fellow citizens causing us untold damage in delicate circumstances abroad. Although this is a vast overstatement of the situation, everyone who has studied our relations with the world agrees that, at all levels of authority, we urgently need many more sensitive and skilled representatives.

CHAPTER XIX

The Framework of Foreign Policy

WHAT course of action will enable us to regain the initiative in our dealings with the Communist nations and place our relations with the non-Communist people of the world on a more enduring basis?

Obviously no *one* line of action will do this. What is required is a co-ordination of political action, economic action and military readiness – all fitting into a new and cohesive American view of the world, a view that reflects our national purpose.

This expression of our national purpose must be worthy of our best historical convictions and of our democratic beliefs.

It must do justice to both our short-term and long-term objectives in world affairs.

It must refresh our impulses for public creative action,

which, since the days of the Marshall Plan, NATO and Point Four, have generally fallen into disuse.

It must involve not only the enunciation of great truths but the initiation of great action, reflected in day-to-day policies, appropriations and administration.

This requires us to rethink the whole nature of the present world crisis and to bring our objectives into the closest possible harmony with those of non-Communist peoples everywhere.

What, then, shall our terms of reference be?

Many American leaders, in and out of government, view the Cold War as a struggle between the American and Russian ways of life, one of which all nations sooner or later must choose. This interpretation places us at a supreme disadvantage.

Whether we like it or understand it, a clear majority of the non-Communist people of the world are unprepared to accept the American way of life as their model.

Most of them are coloured and they resent the continued racial discrimination that exists in much of America.

Most of them are poor, and they are unsympathetic to what impresses them as the arrogance of American wealth.

Most of them are deeply religious and family-oriented by centuries of custom and upbringing, and consequently deplore our soaring statistics of crime, divorce and juvenile delinquency.

To call upon the non-Communist two-thirds of mankind to join us in a crusade for the 'American Way of Life' is therefore self-defeating and futile. It also betrays a narrowly mistaken view of what the world struggle is all about.

This conflict, which now absorbs so much of our resources and energies, goes far beyond the differences between America and the Soviet Union. It is a conflict between those who believe in the dignity of the individual and those who would deny him that dignity.

Our primary task, therefore, is to rally other non-Communist peoples in the common defence of certain primary principles of human conduct which are deeply rooted in most religions and which have provided the central driving force for human freedom and betterment since the beginning of time.

Unless we thus deliberately place our national interests in this context, and unless we learn to act in behalf of our interests in the broadest and most generous terms, we will almost surely fail to secure those interests. Lacking this broader perspective, we will fail to associate our vital long-term objectives with the objectives of our potential friends even when their security and ours are in fact totally tied together.

On the other hand, once we lift our efforts above self-centredness and day-to-day expediency, we will see that the common ground between ourselves and most of the rest of the non-Communist world is enormous. This common ground includes points which are basic to our national purpose, and which reflect on a world scale the promise of the American Dream.

We all seek a genuine peace in which the world gradually can come to live in harmony and understanding.

We seek to build and maintain the political foundations of stable, responsible governments, free of foreign interference and dedicated to the rights of the individual.

We seek to establish the economic conditions on a global scale which eventually will free all people from poverty, illiteracy, and ill health.

We seek to implement these objectives in concert with others, utilizing to the maximum possible degree the machinery of the United Nations and its specialized agencies.

We seek, inside and outside the United Nations, to strengthen respect for law and to hasten the growth of law in the world community.

An international policy squarely and consistently based on these five points automatically becomes more than an American policy. It is also more than an anti-Communist policy. It comes close to being a policy for all humanity. Such a policy alone will provide us with an honest and unassailable position from which to deal with future events.

In 1961, a new national leadership will be confronted with the difficult task of spelling out these essential first principles in practical policy terms. The first consideration will be the question of peace. Everyone agrees that this is the primary need. Unless we can move off our present tightrope of terror, the future of civilization will continue to hang in the balance.

Yet there is grave danger that out of our frustration with the complex challenge which we face, we Americans will come to accept the present Cold Peace as the genuine article. Indeed, this is precisely what much of the world fears has already happened.

At present the 'peace' is preserved by a common, nuclear terror. Our disdain for the judgment or good intentions of our adversaries in Moscow is equalled only by their disdain for ours. Yet the survival of our world rests precariously on the possibility (I cannot believe it is a probability) that the present balance of forces and wills can somehow continue indefinitely without a deadly miscalculation in one camp or the other.

Even if this miscalculation is miraculously avoided the Cold War has created pressures within our society that sooner or later will profoundly affect our perspective, values and objectives.

Military and political judgments in the Pentagon are the decisive economic factor in thousands of American communities. Great American universities look increasingly to the same source for the bulk of their research money and indeed for much of their general income. Millions of young Americans are growing up who have known nothing but Cold War tensions, Cold War materialism, and Cold War political sterility.

Our primary national objective, therefore, is to replace the present Cold Peace preserved by terror with a genuine peace in which fear of war gradually disappears.

Yet here is the heart of our dilemma. A genuine peace can only be achieved by negotiation, and a successful adjustment of the *major* issues between the Atlantic nations and the Communist bloc appears unlikely under present conditions.

Local adjustments may be made, as in the Austrian peace treaty, and perhaps in regard to Berlin, where both sides come to see that their interests are best served by eliminating a specific source of conflict. The present thaw in personal give and take at the summit may be extended.

As for the larger question, however, both the Soviet and the Chinese Communists seem to feel that it is they who hold the long-range military, political and economic advantage. Barring some unexpected development within the Moscow–Peking bloc itself, this means that no settlement of the fundamental issues can be expected for some time.

This brings our task into clear focus. Our objective must be to *create* the global conditions which at some future stage will make possible some meaningful and enforceable agreements. This requires of us a carefully balanced effort in the fields of military defence, economic policy and diplomatic manoeuvre, carried forward within a framework that is consistent with the five objectives previously discussed. It will not be accomplished overnight.

CHAPTER XX

The Role of Military Power

OUR first urgent requirement, as we move to create the conditions in which broad agreements may become possible, is a military force that is sufficient to persuade the men of Moscow and Peking that they cannot hope to gain their ends by force or by threat of force. And to our military strength, there must be added a demonstrable will to use the weapons at hand if matters should reach that point.

On this issue, many non-Communist nations which have

not been subject to Soviet military pressure will almost certainly fail to see eye to eye with us. The solution is not to scold them for what we consider their naïveté, but to proceed without threats or sabre-rattling to build the strength necessary for the task.

Many qualified and persuasive observers, such as Senators Symington and Jackson, and former State Department policy-planning director Paul Nitze, seriously doubt that we now possess such strength, in spite of the fact that we have spent $250 billion since the end of the Korean War, which is equivalent to $1,300 for every man, woman and child in America, to secure it.

The full facts on defence matters are obscure for many reasons. These include the conflicts among the three armed services for priorities on available public funds; the related competition of the highly organized Pentagon publicists; the pressures of industrial interests for certain weapon systems in which they have an economic stake; the struggles for partisan electioneering advantages on the defence issue; the top secret stamp which even the most innocuous national security matters tend to wear; and the sheer scientific and technological complexity of the questions to be judged.

In July 1959, Hanson Baldwin, the distinguished military expert for the *New York Times*, wrote :

The pressures generated within the Pentagon and in Washington by the billions of dollars expended annually for defence are enormous and have been growing. Hence the charge of a munitions lobby.

Local Chambers of Commerce, municipal, and state officials, labour unions, industrial associations, the industries concerned and the Congressmen representing the affected areas all combine to exert pressures in favour of their own areas.

When a missile may be threatened with cancellation or cutback, the call-to-arms is like a tocsin. The missile's value is advertised – sometimes at the expense of the taxpayer. Congressional delegations and public opinion are mobilized and economic bogymen are invoked. Calm, non-partisan and technical judgments become difficult.

Yet sufficient truth penetrates the political haze to make it clear that our present military strength is not fully adequate to our purpose.

Even if it were better planned, contracted for, organized and allocated, it would still not be fully adequate.

If this assumption is correct and if the Kremlin's effort to negotiate us out of Middle Europe and the Middle East fails, Soviet leaders may ultimately come to feel that they can afford to risk a more adventuresome diplomacy.

I have already suggested that earlier NATO strategy, which was sound at the time of its formulation, has been invalidated in two ways :

First, by the fact that the build-up of ground forces in NATO's vital central army has fallen far short of the original plans.

Second, by the fact that Russia has not only broken the American monopoly on the means of delivering nuclear weapons to their targets, but in the next few years may dangerously exceed our own capabilities in this respect.

This means that in the event of attack, our retaliatory power, in theory at least, could be largely knocked out before we could use it. The mere fact that our allies and friends know this to be true could be exploited by a reckless but determined Kremlin to win sweeping diplomatic victories without firing a shot.

Yet the military requirements go beyond the urgent need to maintain nuclear parity with the U.S.S.R.

Such a balance will persuade the Kremlin that it cannot bring its strategic nuclear weapons into play without experiencing a devastating retaliatory attack, and thus in turn will reduce the effective use of massive nuclear power as diplomatic blackmail. But it will not guarantee against the possibility of a ghastly miscalculation, nor will it end the danger of overt aggression by Communist land forces.

The Russians have carefully maintained, modernized and mechanized the 175 divisions of the Red Army. This enables them to bring unlimited ground forces to bear in a single critical area with the knowledge that we lack the mobile forces to meet the threat on a local basis.

They may reasonably assume that we would be unlikely to counter this limited aggression by a major *nuclear* attack that would result in Soviet retaliation against our own cities and in the estimated death of some fifty million Americans.

What course of action in this extraordinarily complex situation commends itself to common sense?

We must not only restore our declining balance of nuclear weapons, but at the same time we must modernize and reinvigorate our conventional armed forces, which were dangerously reduced at the very time when the nuclear advantage was passing from our hands.

This means a new flow of scientific and military invention to increase the fire power of our ground forces and to improve their capacity to hold or slow down any hostile military action directed against our interests.

This, in turn, calls for a new military perspective that will cut through the inefficiency and confusion which observers agree now exists within our military establishment.

Another paper reorganization of the Pentagon will not in itself solve the problem. Ways must be found to eliminate backbiting among the services, to decrease the pressures of various lobbies in behalf of obsolescent weapons and strategies, to cut out duplication, and to move full steam ahead on the balanced defence measures which are necessary to convince our Communist adversaries that neither a large nor a small war is worth the cost.

CHAPTER XXI

The Problems of Disarmament

MEANWHILE, it is absolutely essential that we proceed to negotiate seriously, soberly and exhaustively for ways to end the arms race.

Like the rest of mankind, we Americans deeply fear a catastrophic nuclear miscalculation. We are concerned over the almost daily dose of Strontium 90 which nuclear-weapons testing has contributed to the atmosphere in each of our neighbourhoods.

We also share the impatience of mankind over the human folly which has led presumably civilized nations into an armament race that has absorbed a huge segment of their human and physical resources. It is essential, therefore, that we demonstrate in graphic ways our willingness to explore every reasonable approach to a disarmament agreement.

Although a world-wide nuclear test ban with suitable controls would not in itself reduce armaments, it would provide an invaluable precedent for broader progress. What practical hope do we have for such progress?

There are two potent reasons why it would appear logical for the Kremlin to press for a sweeping disarmament agreement.

First, the Soviet Union could divert savings in military expenditures directly to the expansion of its consumer production, with immediate advantage at home and abroad.

Second, according to Kremlin dogma, the prosperity of the capitalist West is largely dependent on its armament industries. It follows that disarmament would lead to our economic collapse.

As for the first reason, something like twenty-two per cent of the Soviet Union's productive energies is now allocated to the military. With a gross national product of about $200 billion, this is equivalent to more than $40 billion annually.

A general disarmament agreement would enable the Kremlin planners to divert most of this vast sum to other activities that would enormously strengthen the Soviet position. Inside the Soviet Union, massive attacks could be launched on the grave housing shortage. The production of Soviet automobiles and other consumer goods could be increased rapidly. Showplaces could be created to awe and impress foreign visitors with the accomplishments of Communism.

Simultaneously, the Kremlin could launch a subsidized export offensive to undercut the trading position of the capitalist powers in the underdeveloped continents, and, indeed, in Europe itself. Communism, Mr Khrushchev never ceases to tell us, would surely win in any such head-on test in peaceful competition.

As for the second reason why greater Russian interest in disarmament would seem plausible, the Communists assert that as American armament industries closed down, unemployment would rise, and purchasing power would dry up. Rapidly spreading depression would lead to bankruptcies, privation and bitter political differences which would hasten the collapse of capitalism and the coming of the Communist triumph.

Although this Marxist analysis greatly overstates our problem, even the most confirmed of us capitalists must agree that a major reduction in armament spending would create substantial difficulties for American industry.

Why, then, has the Kremlin refused to negotiate in any meaningful way? Although it has issued broadsides, waved banners and released peace doves, it has failed to come up with positive, workable proposals. Why?

The forces at work on disarmament policy within the Soviet Union are necessarily matters of guesswork. But war or peace may ultimately depend upon these guesses. I believe that an explanation of present Soviet behaviour must include some or all of these factors :

1. The assumption on the part of the Kremlin, which we discussed in the previous chapter, that its growing military advantage may be translated into bloodless diplomatic victories.

2. A genuine fear among the Soviet leaders of the very forces which they themselves have brought into being – a resurgent, armed Germany, NATO, and the world-wide American nuclear base system.

3. Six hundred and fifty million dynamic, land-hungry Chinese neighbours, who sooner or later seem likely to bid for leadership in the International Communist movement.

4. The extent to which the Soviet leaders themselves are victims of the Russian tradition of secrecy, and the relative advantages secrecy gives them in an armament race with our more open society.

5. Policy hesitations and conflicting pressures, which may limit the Kremlin's freedom of action as similar differences limit our government's disarmament position. These differences may exist within the Communist party itself and between it and the armed forces.

6. Fear of the impact on the Soviet political system of a relaxation in the Cold War.

This latter point, I believe, may be of particular importance. Following the easing of tensions after the Big Four meeting in Geneva in 1955, the belief spread throughout the Communist empire that the attainment of freedom was within the realm of possibility. This resulted in a near explosion in Poland and a bloody uprising in Hungary.

As the Kremlin saw the raw temper of the occupied nations of Eastern Europe so furiously expressed by this public reaction, it must have been profoundly shaken by the possibility that in a relaxed and disarmed world its empire would disintegrate.

Under the circumstances, what ought we to do? The answer is difficult. Since our estimates of Soviet intentions can be based only on guesswork, we must be prepared, as well as we can be, for any eventuality. I suggest, therefore, that our policy should be threefold:

1. We should prepare for the most extreme possibility – that Russian leaders are not only determined to dominate the world but are preparing to do so by force.

Many observers assert that Soviet reluctance to consider disarmament with genuine safeguards – for instance, the intransigence for months at Geneva even on the limited subject of a control system for nuclear tests – is proof that the Kremlin plans a war at a time and place of its own choosing. In the absence of better evidence to the contrary, we should not take the chance that these Cassandras are wrong.

In the more likely event that Soviet reluctance to disarm is based on a variety of *internal* factors, there is an outside chance that a decision by our government to match the Kremlin missile for missile might persuade the Russian leaders that the race has become too expensive and too dangerous, and that a gradual step-by-step disarmament would be in their interest.

2. At the same time, we must persuade world opinion that we are willing and anxious to negotiate a meaningful disarmament agreement here and now, and that only the Kremlin stands in the way.

On this score we have failed completely. If our present national leadership has a clear, dependable, negotiable policy in regard to such disarmament, no one knows what it is.

The fact that the Soviet Union is unlikely to confront us with a workable plan does not excuse our failure to think through the infinitely complex requirements and to develop a hard-headed series of proposals that we can press steadily and constructively across the negotiating tables and before world opinion.

A realistic approach to disarmament must consider the interests and ambitions of the swaggering Communist government in Peking. We cannot indefinitely disregard the presence on this planet of 650 million militant Chinese, whose leaders, in the absence of some enforceable agreement, will sooner or later possess nuclear weapons.

3. Finally, we must consider the effect on our own society if Russia and China eventually become willing to negotiate a broad disarmament agreement with acceptable inspection safeguards.

This underscores the need for a searching appraisal of the economic impact of disarmament. Karl Marx to the contrary, I believe that our fears on this score are grossly overdone. Although the transition would not be easy, I believe it could be made much more smoothly than most Americans assume.

In 1945, as a member of the War Production Board, I participated in planning our economic transition from war to peace.

Within eighteen months we switched some forty-five per cent of American industry from wartime to peacetime production and absorbed nearly ten million men from our armed services into civilian life.

To be sure, we had the advantage then of a heavy backlog of war-accumulated demands for housing, schools and consumer durables.

But today, the percentage of our economy devoted to defence production is only one-fifth of what it was in 1945. As for our backlog of unfilled needs, every mayor, city planner, educator, highway engineer, hospital superintendent and sociologist knows that they are enormous.

The Senate Disarmament Subcommittee has already conducted pioneer hearings on the economic implications of disarmament. I am convinced that further public reports on this subject would be reassuring to the American people and proof to the world that it is the Soviet Union and not the United States that stands in the way of a realistic reduction of Cold War tensions.

Once we decide the military and political steps that we are prepared to take to lessen the present danger of war, and consider frankly the economic implications of this programme within our own society, our position before the world will be unassailable.

Finally, the world has an immediate and desperate need for effective leadership toward an agreement that will curtail the spread of nuclear weapons and information to additional governments beyond those who now have them.

Competent American experts estimate that there are at least eighteen nations whose economic capacity will enable them to manufacture nuclear weapons during the next decade. The 'nth country problem' leads us into new, enormous dangers, and no initiative for peace can ignore the fantastic problem caused by multiplying the number of the world's nuclear powers.

To what extent, if at all, the Kremlin would be swayed by a new American initiative and a comprehensive American peace policy that considered all the military, political and economic aspects of our current armament situation, no man can say. Changes within the Soviet Union have been considerable since Stalin's death and undoubtedly there are more to come.

Yet, regardless of what the Kremlin says, an affirmative and hard-headed American disarmament position, from which we are prepared to negotiate in good faith, is a continuing national responsibility.

The great powers are now caught up in an awesome, tragic circle. Every move we make to break free involves a delicate balancing of risks. There is no sure, safe course.

It will require both vision and courage to find our way to more solid ground. But the price of running the arms race to its ultimate end is almost certain oblivion. Next time, there will be not one Rome, but two Carthages.

Therefore, let there be no doubt on any continent of America's earnest desire to free the world of nuclear fall-out and to eliminate the awesome possibility that someone, some day, in a moment of panic or rage will pull the fatal trigger.

CHAPTER XXII

What Happens Behind the Barrier

AS I HAVE pointed out, the new Administration which assumes responsibility for American foreign policy in January 1961 faces a twofold task.

First, it must build a tough but flexible defence barrier that will persuade the Communist powers that either a massive Soviet nuclear attack or a localized aggression by Soviet or Chinese ground forces would be doomed to fail.

Second, it must adopt economic and political policies which will encourage the growth of free, friendly non-Communist societies behind that barrier.

No one who understands the massive capacity of the American people, their resources and their economic system will doubt our physical ability to do what is required of us. This leaves only the question of our understanding and will.

If we are to work in effective co-operation with other non-Communist peoples in pursuit of common objectives, we must be deeply sensitive to their hopes and fears. We must also achieve a new sense of humility in regard to our own liabilities and limitations.

The Marshall Plan and the Point Four programme wisely called for a partnership to create the political, economic and social conditions on which free institutions depend. This goal looked far beyond narrow anti-Communism. It looked creatively and positively to the objectives that all free peoples hold in common.

Once we broadly reaffirm this identity between American interests and those of most of the non-Communist world, we can set up standards for granting aid that will make practical sense in concrete situations. And this includes both military and economic aid.

No responsible man will suggest that we recklessly repudiate old agreements; nor can we deny ourselves the right and the means to be highly pragmatic in what we do in special emergency situations. Yet we must never lose sight of our central aim, which is to help the less developed nations create the conditions for freedom.

This means that their people must develop a personal stake in the survival of their governments. They must come to believe that their leaders are genuinely anxious and able to help them protect and promote their interests, and that they will receive justice at their hands. They must experience a sense of direct *participation* in the process of government, thereby erasing the psychological legacy of colonial rule where the government was invariably referred to as 'they', never as 'we'.

Once we understand these essential, primary requirements for a viable nation, we will be in a better position, at the request of the people and governments concerned, to support the initiative they themselves take on many fronts.

This includes their programmes to raise the level of literacy.

It includes land reform measures so that a higher percentage of the land will be efficiently used for food production, while more individual farmers will have the satisfaction of owning their own property.

It includes the development of a free, responsible labour movement, to lessen the explosive gap between rich and poor.

It includes community development projects in the rural areas to help increase food production, improve distribution, control disease, build roads and schools and create small village industries.

It includes training in the technique of modern public administration so that the new governments will not only be efficient in a mechanistic sense, but will also respect the need for individual freedom.

The most important standard for granting American economic loans and other assistance should be the recipient nations' readiness to commit themselves to a programme of hard work and self-sacrifice. That is to say, American grants or loans for substantial long-term assistance should go primarily to those countries that are making a major, honest effort to finance their own national development from their own resources; countries that are striving to serve the interests of the many, not simply those of the fortunate ruling group.

The Republic of India is a dramatic example of a great underdeveloped nation which is making this very effort. Though India is underdeveloped, it is rapidly coming into its own as a major power with great influence and potential.

It is a subcontinent comparable to Europe in area and population and even richer in resources. Indeed, the population of the single Indian state of Uttar Pradesh exceeds that of Italy, France, Germany or the United Kingdom. India's population of 400 million nearly equals the population of Africa and South America combined.

Through a tough, well-administered tax system and equally stringent controls on luxury imports, India has demonstrated its willingness to make major sacrifices on its own behalf. Moreover, India inherited an outstanding, British-trained civil service, the most efficient in Asia, and it has kept that service at a high degree of competence.

Already India has completed one five-year plan and in 1960 will be nearly through her second. A third such plan – for which American, British, German, Japanese and Canadian assistance will be sorely needed – will be launched shortly after our new Administration takes office in January 1961.

Finally, in the eyes of Asians, India stands today as the one political and economic alternative to the path being followed by Communist China. If the Indian democratic experiment fails, whatever long-range hope may exist for the growth of free democratic societies in the vast arc between Tokyo and Casablanca probably falls with it.

For all these practical reasons, I believe that India should be assured the intensive, long-term investment and technical support it needs to meet its economic development objectives.

Countries like Pakistan, the Philippines, Formosa, Vietnam, Israel, Ghana, Tunisia, Chile, Costa Rica and several others could also meet the standards I have in mind.

As still other countries approach these criteria, and as we see that more long-term aid can effectively be used by them, they too should receive from us the special kind of extra help they need.

Countries which are now unable to meet minimum development standards should tactfully be told that they cannot expect major investment assistance from us until they have created their own internal basis for successful growth.

This does not mean that we should turn our backs on them. On the contrary, there is much that we can and should do to help.

We should offer to assist them in the creation of a comprehensive economic development plan which enables them to use their own resources to the best possible advantage.

We should help provide tax experts, engineering survey teams, and other technicians to create a workable administrative base.

We should urge them to inaugurate land reforms and suggest expert advisers to help them. American governmental experts assigned to Japan and Formosa led in promoting a programme of private land ownership whereby the peasants in these two countries have set records in agricultural productivity and in a general expansion of rural democracy.

More specifically and immediately, we can help these nations finance individual projects that are worth while in their own right, that are not dependent on the economy of the country as a whole, and that are clearly in the people's interest.

An example might be a modern hospital in the national capital, with training facilities for doctors and nurses and an outpatient clinic system for the villages; or an expanded and improved university or agricultural experiment college.

It is true, of course, that no set of criteria can solve all the practical day-to-day problems of allocating American economic assistance. Special economic help, usually labelled 'defence support', is sometimes needed to meet unusual political situations. It may also be needed to provide economic services that backstop a military programme or insure the effectiveness of a critically important military base.

But while admitting the need for the foregoing, let us not confuse such aid with constructive developmental assistance. Let us recognize it as a temporary expedient, self-limiting in time and object.

American diplomacy should be equal to the task of persuading other nations that mutual security is, as its name implies, a two-way *partnership*. That means that our representatives should make it plain that we will not be pressured indefinitely into paying for the privilege of building military installations that are designed to protect the nation in which the base is located as well as ourselves.

It may be suggested that any selective standards we apply to the distribution of American economic aid will be resented by many friendly nations as 'political interference'. Although some such criticism undoubtedly will be made, we should not regard it as unanswerable.

Tactful American negotiators, supported by a firm Congressional mandate, can convince most governments that such criteria are essential in their own long-range interests as well as in ours.

Over and beyond all this, there are other steps to be taken which would substantially increase the effectiveness of our economic development assistance. To mention but a few :

Wherever practicable we should strive to channel economic aid and particularly technical aid through international agencies.

In many areas, United Nations aid is more acceptable than our own. Moreover, United Nations administrators and other international civil servants are often in a better position to press recipient governments toward the changes in their tax, trading or planning policies that are important to the success of their development programmes. The best evidence of this can be seen in the unique position the World Bank enjoys in the eyes of the underdeveloped countries.

We also need a continuing source of credit for nations which cannot repay their loans with hard currencies.

The Development Loan Fund was formed in 1957 to make loans to less-developed countries which are waiting to start work on sound economic projects but which can't qualify for loans from private or other government sources. In the case of the Fund, loans are repayable either in local foreign currency or in dollars and at much lower interest rates than are available elsewhere.

The performance of the Development Loan Fund has been impressive. It can also do even more if it is adequately capitalized and placed on a long-term basis.

We must also search for new ways to bring private American investment capital and American industrial management to bear on the problems of world development.

During most of the long *Pax Britannica,* when Britain largely maintained the peace of the world, the British invested overseas at least ten per cent of their gross national product every year and a sizeable percentage of their ablest men and women.

The situation, of course, was different then. In nineteenth-century Britain there was neither income nor corporation tax. This meant that substantially greater private savings were available for overseas investment. More than that, the areas into which British investments were channelled were under tight enough colonial controls to eliminate the *political* risks.

Today, in the face of the political risks which inevitably go with our revolutionary age, imaginative new administrative and legislative techniques must be developed to encourage American executive experience and capital to play a larger role in serving our national objectives in world affairs.

This will be a primary task for the new Administration that takes office in January 1961.

CHAPTER XXIII

The Need for Able People

THE success of every public policy depends in large measure on the people who are assigned to carry it out. This is doubly true of foreign policy, which involves so many sensitive human relations and attitudes.

As I have suggested in an earlier chapter, American representatives do not always measure up to standards which are imperative for the success of American policy.

In the exciting, creative atmosphere of the Marshall Plan and Point Four, thousands of able and dedicated men joined our embassies, economic missions and information services overseas.

In the intensely partisan atmosphere following the election of 1952, thousands of these people were purged. As the heart went out of the effort, thousands more became frustrated and finally drifted back to businesses, law practices and universities.

In the winter of 1959, when the President was asked at his press conference to comment on yet another turnover in foreign aid administrators, he replied in a discouraged mood : 'That's one that after a while everybody gets worn down about. . . . They have a very hostile type of atmosphere in which to do their testifying and to seek their appropriations.

'It is a very worrisome job that they have and I can't blame them much, although I hate to lose Mr Smith [the departing administrator], and I don't know who I am going to get to take his place.'

Recently the atmosphere has been improved. Major credit for this is due to Secretary Herter and Under-Secretary Dillon, who have done so much to restore the morale and competence of our overseas organizations.

However, we must do much more.

Our embassies are largely manned by experienced, hard-working Foreign Service officers. Yet Chiefs of Mission are often hampered by a tradition of social exclusiveness and artificiality which contributes in considerable degree to the very public impression which we and they are most anxious to avoid.

This tradition has placed too much emphasis on the glamorous entertaining of the capital elite and too little on the embassy's more vital tasks, including the primary need for getting to know the country and its people.

This over-emphasis on the social requirements, compounded by our failure to provide adequate entertainment allowances for such socially demanding embassies as London, Paris and Rome, has mistakenly led us to accept the appointment of wealthy political contributors to represent us in some of the world's most important capitals.

This is not to argue against the selection of non-career ambassadors to supplement our career service. Although some extremely unwise appointments have been made, the policy of appointing non-career ambassadors has also produced some of our ablest Chiefs of Mission in recent years.

The examples include Mrs Eugenie Anderson of Minnesota, who won the heart of Denmark as our Ambassador there; Douglas Dillon, former Ambassador to France; John J. McCloy, former High Commissioner in Germany; David K. E. Bruce, our recent Ambassador to Bonn; George McGhee, who represented us so ably in Turkey; and many others.

These and other distinguished public servants, both Repub-

licans and Democrats, have brought a freshness of view and
a courage of expression to our Foreign Service that have been
invaluable.

Yet the choice of an ambassador should not be determined
or even influenced by his personal income. If our embassy in
Paris, Rome or London calls for the talents of a particular
career Foreign Service diplomat, his living and entertainment
allowances should be sufficient to enable him to take the
assignment.

The well-publicized financial demands of diplomatic life
should not, however, obscure the much more fundamental
question of ambassadorial responsibilities. Even more than
bigger embassy allowances, we need bigger *concepts* on what
our American ambassadors are supposed to do.

What precisely are the requirements?

Traditionally, the American ambassador, as senior representative in the country of his assignment, provides the State
Department with a flow of comprehensive reports on political,
economic and social developments in that country. He
negotiates bilateral agreements. He acts as America's representative at official functions. He assists American business
firms.

He directs his own political and economic staff, and has
general supervisory responsibility for the United States Information Service, and for whatever American economic and
military missions may be at work in the country to which he
is accredited.

These routine demands on his time, energies and talents are
of the utmost importance. Yet his role in today's world should
go far beyond that of an able observer, reporter, negotiator
and official representative at high-level dinners and teas.

An ambassador should develop a deep, sensitive, personal
understanding of the country of his assignment. This understanding must go far beyond its governmental institutions, its
history, and the financial, diplomatic and military elite of the

national capital. It must include the peasants, workers, school-teachers, students and bazaar keepers whose ideas, hopes and prejudices will ultimately shape their country's future.

It is also his responsibility to help make our own country, our people and our objectives understandable to men and women of varied backgrounds and experience, most of whom will be dubious and many antagonistic.

Only if he accepts this broader understanding of his role will he be able to move beyond the narrow limits of conventional diplomacy to influence constructively the course of events.

The Administration which takes office in January 1961 will face many critical tasks. But none will be more important than to restore to those governmental services dealing with world affairs the sense of high purpose and unselfish commitment that existed during the war and immediately after the war.

Once this has been done, able men and women will again be clamouring to serve their government and their country in this promising and dangerous age.

There remains one final point : How can we improve our overseas information programmes? The key lies in the philosophy of foreign relations which we have been considering throughout these chapters.

If we associate our national objectives more closely with those of the non-Communist two-thirds of mankind, and if our day-to-day policies and actions reflect the principles that brought us to greatness under Jefferson, Jackson, Lincoln, Wilson and Roosevelt – then our global public relations problem will rapidly become more manageable.

Advertising experts tell their clients that 'even the best advertising cannot sell a bad product twice'. Their efforts to sell American policies in various parts of the world have often failed because they disregarded this very principle.

What they call the American 'image' has often come through militaristic, slick, arrogant and rich. In country after country, the real America has been obscured in a fog of press statements and radio broadcasts better designed to flatter Americans at home than to persuade foreigners abroad.

A new Administration will have its work cut out to bring our informational efforts abroad into better balance. Yet once we begin to do the right things and say the right things, once we send more sensitive and able Americans abroad and recall those whose antics and attitudes reflect adversely on our country, the work of the United States Information Service will become vastly easier.

The foreign policy challenge which I have outlined is vast and urgent. If we are adequately to meet it by building up our defence security barrier and taking more affirmative action to build viable free societies behind that barrier, our machinery of government must be geared for the task.

At present our national effort is hampered by the conflict-ridden Pentagon, by the overlapping authority of agencies dealing with economic aid, and by the need for better liaison as well as wider agreement on fundamentals between the State Department, Bureau of the Budget, and the Departments of the Treasury, Commerce and Agriculture. This situation will present the new administration with a formidable challenge.

However, overlapping and conflicting Congressional responsibilities have also contributed heavily to our policy-making difficulties. Although a dozen or more Senate and House committees deal in one way or another with foreign policy problems, few of them share a common perspective or even common facts.

The National Security Council was set up to co-ordinate foreign policy-making in the executive branch of our government. A comparative legislative body, perhaps a joint committee of outstanding Congressional leaders from both the Senate and the House, is urgently needed on Capitol Hill.

Such a committee could help mightily to provide the long range legislative perspective and responsibility which are essential as we move into a new era of American foreign policy.

CHAPTER XXIV

Can Democracy Measure Up?

Is it possible for a free-wheeling democracy of 180 million people to develop, support and sustain an effective foreign policy in today's complicated world?

More than a century ago de Tocqueville, in referring to a world of far simpler dimensions, expressed grave doubts about the capacity of democratic governments successfully to conduct foreign affairs. This critical area of government, he argued, called for qualities more readily associated with an aristocracy than with the representatives of a democratic people.

Several thoughtful American observers have recently echoed similar forebodings. An effective foreign policy, they assert, can best be conducted by specially trained and conditioned experts free of the often illogical swings of democratic public opinion.

The skill with which the elite in the British Foreign Office guided Britain's foreign policy through the long century of peace prior to the outbreak of World War I is often offered as a case in point.

Although substantial grounds exist for these pessimistic views, the evidence is not all in one direction. Indeed, our brilliant response to the unprecedented situation which faced us in Europe following the war justifies a large measure of confidence in our potential power to devise good policies, secure public and Congressional support, and administer them with boldness and political skill.

Moreover, in England's own case, it is worth pointing out that the Oxford–Cambridge elite which directed Britain's foreign policy in the nineteenth century did not work in hermetically sealed chambers cut off from the winds of public opinion.

On the contrary, it acted within the framework of a remarkably consistent public consensus in foreign policy which had developed in England over a period of years.

This consensus was based on the practical experiences of several generations of Englishmen. The dock worker in Liverpool, the cotton weaver in Manchester, the miner in Wales, and the shopkeeper in London were in basic agreement about British national interests and how Britain could best defend and advance those interests. This in turn enabled the architects of British foreign policy to plan and act with confidence.

The broadly accepted national consensus to which I refer embraced three generally understood, deeply rooted British objectives for which the British people were always prepared to fight.

1. Freedom of the seas for British trade.

2. The integrity of the Empire and the preservation of its lifelines, particularly those leading to India through the Middle East.

3. The maintenance of a military power balance between the nations of Europe.

Any British government that acted within this general framework could operate boldly and affirmatively with the assurance of public support.

This is not to say that foreign policy questions were not, on occasion, debated with vehemence in the House of Commons, Hyde Park and elsewhere. The deep division on Irish freedom is a case in point. The British Foreign Office's support for the South during the American Civil War is another. Indeed, in the latter case British public opinion, which strongly opposed slavery, forced a reversal.

Does a national consensus of this kind exist in America today?

If we listen to the babble of contradictory voices in our national capital, the answer would appear to be in the negative. Yet Washington is not America.

In the last several years, I have visited most states and discussed American foreign policy with groups that form a cross-section of our society. This experience has left me profoundly convinced that a new consensus of foreign policy has already been reached. Inarticulate and uncertain, it is awaiting only a fresh and affirmative leadership that will call upon the American people to play their vital role.

Let me briefly sketch the principal points of this evolving consensus as I see it.

For one thing, Americans earnestly, urgently want peace. They are uneasy about adventures in brinkmanship.

Yet they know that peace cannot be secured by a wobbly defence or uncertain nerves in the face of aggression. They are therefore prepared to support positive action by their government in opposition to such aggression.

Having rejected isolationism, the American people have also come to understand their economic interrelation with the world. Although they are bombarded by high-tariff arguments and by the most bitter and often demagogic opposition to foreign aid, and their national leadership on these questions has fluctuated between apathy and confusion, the public opinion polls show that their support for a reasonable, low-tariff policy and for more adequate economic aid is substantial.

The American people also seek a responsible liquidation of the last vestiges of colonialism. Algeria is a case in point.

Most Americans feel a deep regard for France. Yet in the marrow of their bones their support on this issue goes to the Algerian rebels with whom they have no personal acquaintance. It is enough for them to know that the struggle there is for national independence.

Finally, there is a growing national agreement that what passes for 'neutralism' in harassed, newly-free nations is not wholly unreasonable. When a man like Nehru, faced with overwhelming internal problems, makes a somewhat equivocal response to Chinese Communist provocations on India's northern border, most Americans are irritated and confused. Yet their understanding of his overriding economic and political priorities grows steadily.

The truth of the matter is that the American people have been quietly arriving at their own evaluations of our new world and its requirements. Despite frequently discordant notes from Washington conference rooms, the agreement among them has become remarkably broad.

The situation is awaiting a new affirmative leadership which will re-establish our world-wide goals in the familiar terms of our American tradition and spell out the policies that fit these objectives.

Such leadership, I believe, will receive overwhelming public support.

PART V

The Party of Hope
or The Party of Memory

There is a mysterious cycle in human events. To some generations much is given. Of other generations much is expected. This generation of Americans has a rendezvous with destiny. . . . We are fighting to save a great and precious form of government for ourselves and for the world.

FRANKLIN DELANO ROOSEVELT

Philadelphia, June 27th, 1936

CHAPTER XXV

The Presidency and the New Consensus

LET us turn now to the political implications of the new national consensus on domestic and foreign policy questions which has been taking shape.

In an earlier chapter we saw that such a consensus does not in itself provide the self-generating power for legislative and executive action. Instead it reflects permissive and often inarticulate public moods within whose framework a new leadership can propose fresh and affirmative lines of action, and anticipate a favourable public response.

We also saw that each previous political breakthrough into a creative new period coincided with an intense public concern over some disturbing new challenge to which old answers appeared inadequate.

Moreover, we saw that in each successful instance where the people responded to a fresh approach, the process did not entail a headlong plunge into uncharted political darkness. Instead it represented a logical extension and refocusing of traditional American beliefs to deal with new situations.

All this serves to raise several questions :

Will the issues involved in this new fourth consensus in our political history be conscientiously debated in the campaign of 1960?

Or will the new consensus become apparent only in the post-election actions of the newly elected President, as was true of the new political eras Lincoln and Roosevelt ushered in?

Or will both political parties miss their present opportunity entirely? Will they – and the rest of us with them – attempt to muddle through four or even eight more sterile years, debating increasingly irrelevant issues while forces capable of destroying our society continue to grow in destructiveness?

We must all fervently hope that the 1960 election will prove to be another one of those historic turning points where, in response to a new challenge, we abandon outdated partisan clichés, unshackle our political dynamism, and refocus our national purpose on the task at hand.

Nor is it altogether wishful thinking to suggest that something of the sort is about to take place.

Even now, the necessary public consensus on domestic and foreign affairs appears largely to be formed. Able leadership which understands its scope may be coming forward in both political parties.

To be sure, we are not on the edge of civil war as in Lincoln's day nor in the midst of a great depression as in Roosevelt's. But the ominous possibility of nuclear catastrophe should be evident to everyone.

The stage therefore appears set for the emergence of a new national leadership which senses that the public is ready for constructive change, and which is prepared to chart a clear course that will enable us again to take charge of our national destiny.

Of political importance, too, is the fact that the new consensus now forming does not represent a radical break with the past. On the contrary, it carries with it a distillation of the best in our American tradition and thus projects a familiar evolutionary line of national policy for the years ahead.

Democracy after all works best when it brings into the bloodstream of public action ideas which have already been filtered through popular understanding. This is precisely what the consensus is now doing.

Thus in defining and stating their political case, our parties need not overreach themselves.

It will be neither wise nor just for either to jar the nation by a sudden call for battle along sharply drawn lines. The important thing for each is to recognize the consensus, know what distinctive proposals it wants to make in this context, and to keep on talking in an open political discussion until the means for action become as much a habit of the heart as of the mind.

We do not want either party to win a monopoly of power in ways that spell the death of its rival. Nor do we want either to hold office so long that it becomes slack and careless, while the party out of power becomes embittered and tempted to resort to increasingly reckless measures in order to win a majority.

We want each to respect the rules of fair play, to be capable of wresting a victory from its rival in ways that will advance instead of imperil the process of orderly government.

This in turn means that each must contain within its ranks liberal-minded men and women who respect their counterparts in the opposition party, and who know how to talk with them in the search for agreement on how the interests of the nation as a whole can be advanced.

Whether we favour one party or the other, we will continue to need them both, each serving in its own way the principle on which our government was founded – in Alexander Hamilton's words, 'power as the rival of power'.

Which brings me to this critical point : despite its lack of explicitness, the new consensus on domestic and foreign policy which I believe is rapidly taking shape, is *already* becoming a habit of the national heart and mind. The evidence lies in the degree to which it has already set the framework of discussion as we move toward the 1960 campaign.

Consider, for example, an imaginary meeting of the Republican and Democratic leaders most prominently mentioned for the Presidential nomination of their parties in 1960.

Seated around the table are Vice-President Richard M. Nixon, Senators Jack Kennedy, Hubert Humphrey, Lyndon Johnson and Stuart Symington, and Governors Adlai Stevenson, Pat Brown, Mennen Williams and Robert Meyner.

Each of us, of course, has his personal and partisan views on which of these nine men may be best qualified to be

President. Yet putting these preferences aside, how sharply divided would their estimates be on the urgent character of America's domestic and foreign needs – and what we can and should do to meet them?

Whether the need is defined in terms of a more versatile defence establishment, a strong peace initiative, bolder economic assistance to the underdeveloped countries, civil rights, or the role of government in an expanding economy, each of the leaders mentioned would profess to see eye to eye on essential principles.

They might also agree that any Presidential aspirant who openly attacked the objectives of the emerging new consensus would almost certainly be defeated, and that in each case their own personal prospects would suffer in the degree to which the voters rightly or wrongly questioned their devotion to those objectives.

Such tactical dilemmas as each contender may feel he has yet to resolve arise from the foregoing reality.

As an illustrative case in point, let us take Vice-President Richard Nixon's position, as the apparent Republican nominee. He knows that he has to overcome the impression, inherited from his early free-wheeling political days, that he is indifferent to human decencies. Accordingly he is straining to identify himself in graphic ways with the cause of civil rights.

Mr Nixon also knows that he is not clearly identified with the cause of an expanding, fully employed America. Since he is a prominent member of an Administration which, in 1960, will have behind it eight years of national economic responsibility, this may prove to be the most difficult political weakness for him to correct.

The timid and restrictive economic notions to which the Administration subscribes have more or less cornered the Vice-President. He will have a hard time extricating himself from the awkwardness of his position, and he knows it.

He cannot openly repudiate the Administration's economic

concepts. Yet if he is unable to identify himself with the public demands for sustained economic growth, without inflation and without these frequent and costly recessions, he may win the nomination only to lose the election.

Meanwhile, in a negative sense, the remarkable similarity between the expressed views of the nine leading candidates for President is underscored by the absence of *any* candidate representing a sharply divergent position.

If a sizable American constituency believed that we should weaken our ties with the United Nations, intensify the Cold War, eliminate foreign aid, raise tariffs, limit the right to strike, reduce Social Security, and curb the Supreme Court, we can be sure that by now articulate, well-financed, Presidential aspirants would eagerly have come forward to represent these views.

But this discordant note has not been struck by any candidate or potential candidate. Conservative leaders in both parties who harbour such views and who still carry great influence inside Congress appear to have reached a new low ebb of *national* political effectiveness.

All this means that Congressional politics is not the same as Presidential politics. Many men in both parties will continue to win elections to House and Senate seats by openly and often bitterly opposing many aspects of the domestic and foreign policy consensus which I have sketched.

In Congressional politics, hundreds of local and regional constituencies choose hundreds of men, each of whom speaks with his own particular appeal on local and regional matters. But in Presidential politics, a national constituency chooses one man who it believes can speak the national voice in national and international matters.

This has created a *Presidential* wing and a *Congressional* wing within both the Republican and Democratic parties. The Presidential wing is primarily oriented toward winning the White House. Its forum in 1960 is the national nominating convention. Of necessity it thinks in national and international terms.

The Congressional wing is primarily oriented toward winning House and Senate seats. Its forum is the Congress proper, where it is often under heavy pressure to put local and state interests above national interests.

These natural pressures have been increased because gerrymandering by state legislatures has led to an over-representation of sparsely settled rural areas in the House at the expense of the great population centres.

More than that, the two houses of Congress function through a complex maze of nearly three hundred committees and subcommittees, whose chairmen are raised to positions of great power by seniority rules. This means they are often elected from safe constituencies with a relatively narrow outlook. The system enables them to shape or even block national legislation from a purely local perspective.

Thus they may and often do take positions on important issues which deviate sharply from the strong tides of opinion that run through the urban centres where Presidential elections are largely decided.

This helps explain why Congress as a whole at times seems to act in ways that are out of touch with what the nation wants done. It also explains why the American people have come to look on the elections of a Congress and a President quite differently.

When we cast a vote for Senator or Representative, our immediate bread-and-butter concerns are usually uppermost in our minds. Primarily, we want to know how this or that candidate, if elected, will serve our immediate personal needs in the national government; how he will vote, for example, on domestic and household matters such as Social Security, veterans' affairs, or that new dam or highway project.

But when we choose a President, our sights are raised beyond the here and now. We look for a man who not only reflects our national domestic needs but who also embodies our highest aspirations to live and grow in peace and friendship within the family of nations.

For the latter reason, foreign policy since 1940 has been the dominant element in the selection of America's Presidents just as it has more recently guided the choice of the chief leaders of Europe's democracies – Macmillan in England, De Gaulle in France and Adenauer in Germany.

In four of our last five Presidential elections the decision emerged from the subconscious and unspoken attitudes of the voters as shaped by their overriding concern about the issues of war and peace.

A brief glance at the record bears this out :

1. In February 1940, there was deep uncertainty about the appropriateness of Franklin D. Roosevelt's running for a third term. The force of the anti-third-term tradition stood in the way of another bid for the White House and many doubted that he could win.

A few months later, however, America was suddenly startled into a new awareness of the world beyond our shores. The Nazi conquest of Norway, Denmark, Belgium, Holland and France and the imminent threat of an assault on England brought a sense of insecurity into almost every American home. And with it came an awareness of the continuing need for experienced leadership in Washington.

Up to this point, the front-running candidates for the Republican Presidential nomination were men who had identified themselves with the cause of isolationism.

To them, Mr Roosevelt's ringing of the international alarm bell seemed but a crude effort to create an artificial sense of emergency that would permit him to continue with his alleged 'usurpations of executive power'.

But when the 1940 Republican National Convention met to the off-stage cries of newsboys shrieking the headline realities of Britain's presumably imminent collapse, the front-running candidates suddenly seemed irrelevant to the needs of the hour.

A few days later the Republican Convention, by-passing the established leadership of their party, gave the Presidential nomination to Wendell Willkie, an attractive world-minded newcomer, who was relatively unhampered by previous commitments.

This had the undoubted effect of narrowing the election-day margin between the Democratic and Republican Presidential candidates. But as the international situation had rapidly grown more dangerous, the American people brushed aside the anti-third-term tradition to keep an experienced President in the White House.

2. In the election of 1944, Governor Thomas E. Dewey, as the Republican challenger for the Presidency, argued that he was better equipped to bring the war to an early and successful conclusion, and to manage the problems of peace that followed.

But once again the decision went to the man most tested in world affairs. Mr Roosevelt's fourth election was a mark of continued public confidence in his capacity as a wartime and peacetime leader.

In the entire course of the campaign he made only one speech on domestic questions. On that occasion he promised a full-production, full-employment economy to the returning veterans.

3. The election of 1948 was the only one of the last five in which foreign-policy questions were not of decisive importance. In the wake of the war, domestic issues such as high prices, lack of schools and housing, and farm problems were paramount in Mr Truman's successful re-election bid.

Nevertheless, few would deny, least of all Mr Truman himself, that his victory received an important assist from his brilliant achievements in foreign policy – the Truman Doctrine, the Marshall Plan, and the initial planning of NATO.

4. In 1952, the Republican Convention faced a choice between Senator Taft and General Eisenhower. As the master of the Republican forces in the Congress, Mr Taft was then

at the peak of his effectiveness. He was the respected party theoretician, tactician and work horse. He was 'Mr Republican'.

General Eisenhower, on the other hand, was a latecomer to the ranks of the Republican party. He had never made a political speech. Indeed, as late as 1948 many had assumed that he was a Democrat.

Yet the cards were stacked in his favour.

Senator Taft suffered from the public conviction that he would return America to isolationism. In contrast General Eisenhower was looked upon as a man of broad experience in a variety of foreign assignments who could be counted on to keep America in the world.

The foreign policy fears surrounding Senator Taft and the foreign policy assurance surrounding the General were the central issues at the 1952 Republican Convention.

The Democratic nominating convention of that year picked Governor Adlai E. Stevenson. Whatever chance Mr Stevenson had of washing out the disadvantage of his party's twenty years in power was destroyed by the General's prompt assumption of the mantle of peace.

5. In 1956 the pattern was repeated: President Eisenhower was presented as the patient negotiator at the Geneva summit meeting, as the sturdy wartime leader whose energies were now devoted to peace.

Indeed, this image appeared so formidable that most Democrats were awed into well-nigh complete silence on the central question which most concerned the people. The Republicans won the foreign policy argument almost by default; and with it, the Presidency.

The growing and already primary importance of foreign policy in selecting our Presidential candidates is almost certain to lessen the traditional eligibility of the governors and to increase that of the Senators, who deal regularly with foreign policy questions.

The knowledge that foreign policy is a decisive influence in determining the outcome of Presidential elections is now shared by all the leading aspirants for the Presidential office. And all are responding to this understanding with remarkably similar appeals to public confidence. A generation or so ago this would not have been possible.

In the 1920's or early 1930's any Presidential candidate would squirm in acute discomfort if his opponents could prove that he was well thought of abroad. Now the exact reverse is the case.

In 1960 all serious candidates for the Presidency must show that they are respected not only by our NATO allies and in the maximum possible number of world capitals, but indeed as far away as Novosibirsk.

CHAPTER XXVI

The Republican Dilemma

FEW Americans believe that either the Republican or Democratic party has a monopoly on virtue or ability. What Macaulay wrote more than one hundred years ago in his *History of England* about two other great parties is relevant to our situation in America today.

> No man utterly destitute of judgment and candour will deny that there are many deep stains on the fame of the party to which he belongs, or that the party to which he is opposed may justly boast of many illustrious names, of many heroic activities, and of many great services rendered the state.
>
> The truth is, though both parties have often seriously erred [the nation] could have spared neither.

If, in her institutions, freedom and order, the advantages rising from innovation and the advantages arising from prescription, have been combined to an extent elsewhere unknown, we may attribute this happy peculiarity to the strenuous conflicts and alternate victories of two rival confederacies of statesmen, a confederacy zealous for authority and antiquity, and a confederacy zealous for liberty and progress.

Which of our own two political parties is most 'zealous for liberty and progress' and therefore best equipped to give form and substance to the new consensus through affirmative national leadership? Which of our two parties is most eligible to qualify in the decisive election of 1960 as the Party of Hope?

To ask this question is to enter the area of political choice and judgment. If what I say is to have practical meaning in this election year, I must speak my convictions with candour as one who has made his own deliberate choice of the Democratic party.

I do not suggest that the Democratic party has always been the exclusive home of the American liberal spirit. To do so would be to oversimplify history. It would also be a gross injustice to the liberal-minded men and women who belong to the Republican party.

Yet the Republican liberals who launched their campaign for 'Modern Republicanism' with such high hopes only seven years ago have seen their purposes frustrated over and over again by the deeply entrenched conservative leaders whose powers of recovery from convention defeats seem unlimited.

This underscores the need to examine not only the quality of both Presidential candidates as they emerge from the nominating conventions, but the characteristics of the party on which each will henceforth depend for his advisers, administrators and legislative support.

All the leading aspirants for the Presidency now in sight may be unusually in accord on what the nation requires and how the requirements can be met. Their sense of emerging history, their mental perceptions, their physical energy, their refreshing eagerness to tap expert staff assistance from colleges and universities, their will to decide and to assume responsibility for the consequences of decisions are of crucial importance.

Yet whoever occupies the White House may be as much the instrument as he is the master of the forces that swirl around him. By all odds the most powerful of these forces are the pressures brought to bear by the political party to which he owes his election.

The Republican party began as a sectional party with a sectional candidate and a sectional programme. And try as it might over the past hundred years, it has not yet been able to establish itself on a truly national basis.

To be sure, it has occasionally carried a few Southern states in Presidential elections. But thus far at least, these successes have been transient.

The Republican party is also primarily a one-interest party which speaks in the main for large corporate concerns. This is not to say that it has no support from farmers, workers and small businessmen. Of course it does. If it did not, it could never have won the Presidency.

But whenever choices must be made between clashing group interests, Republican leaders have traditionally given priority to the wishes of big business. This is true even when the long-term interests of big business have been poorly served by such favourable treatment.

In saying this, I by no means subscribe to the notion that a business civilization is an enemy of the finer things of life.

This is demonstrable nonsense. The great cultures of classical Greece, Rome, Renaissance Italy and Elizabethan England, all arose from business-dominated civilizations and were sustained by them.

The very great prestige which businessmen have won for themselves in America reflects our appreciation of their abilities in organizing production and distribution. It also reflects appreciation for the leisure and national abundance which has flowed from this production.

Therefore, when a responsible observer points out that the Republican party invariably gives priority to short-term business interests, he is not alleging that the Republicans are guilty of a high crime or misdemeanour. The business view is as much entitled to its political voice as the labour, farm or any other view.

The question to be asked is whether the Republican party is serving its *own* interests, let alone the national interest, by giving the claims of business precedence over other equally legitimate claims.

No single interest in America is large enough to form a majority by itself. Judged alongside the total population, each is a minority. It can share in the majority voice only by forming coalitions with other minority interests.

This calls for a sympathetic awareness of the needs of other people; a willingness to go halfway toward meeting them; and an ability to negotiate accommodations between rival minority interests in order to serve the paramount national interest.

A party dominated by a single-interest view – whatever it is – has difficulty in effectively meeting this test of national interest. Indeed, it finds it hard even to serve effectively the interests of the special group to which it gives priority, since in doing this it tends to overlook the long-term needs of the nation of which this group is a part.

Moreover, a political party which gives an almost instinctive priority to the businessman's point of view rarely produces 'politicians in depth'. At best it occasionally produces great but surprising mutations. Teddy Roosevelt, Wendell Willkie, and now Nelson Rockefeller, are examples.

These men broke free from the limitations of their party's views to achieve a more comprehensive grasp of the national interest. Yet the history of the Republican party has demonstrated that when these exceptions do occur, the individual involved generally finds himself isolated from his own party organization.

Now let us consider the preceding generalities in terms of the present Administration. Needless to say, I do not question the character or motives of Mr Eisenhower. He has won the well-merited respect and affection of all Americans, Democrats and Republicans alike. Throughout his career his paramount concern, like that of his Democratic predecessors, has been to serve the nation as a whole – to advance its prosperity at home and the cause of peace abroad.

But what about his performance as a Republican President?

Many of his most devoted supporters admit their disappoint-ment over the ineffectiveness of our national leadership in the seven years since he entered the White House. And many are frank enough to agree that the chief source of the President's difficulties has come from his fellow Republicans.

I believe that historians of this period will substantiate this judgment. At best the Eisenhower Presidency has been under siege from right-wing Republicans, and at worst captured by them.

To make the point in another way, I will add my personal view that the limitations which Mr Eisenhower brought to the Presidency would largely have been overcome had he been elected as a Democratic President. As a Democrat his record would have proved far more substantial, and his place in the political history of America would now be more secure.

Mr Eisenhower's defeat of the well-organized and amply financed Taft forces at the 1952 Republican Convention was an exciting and rewarding television spectacular. The men who managed it were identified with the more liberal wing of their party.

Here, for all the nation to see, was a radiant new oppor-tunity for a resurgence of Republican liberalism in the tradi-tion of Theodore Roosevelt and Wendell Willkie. Here was a chance to reconstruct the Republican party along vibrant new lines, as F.D.R. had reconstructed a somewhat jaded Democratic party after his 1932 election.

Yet soon after his convention victory General Eisenhower, a novice to politics, was persuaded by the diehard forces which he had just defeated in the nominating contest that his primary work was to unite the party, not the nation. Playing from weakness, rather than from his newly won political strength, he hobbled his own good instincts and took his guidance from the professionals.

Words strange to his tongue, but familiar enough as right-wing dogma, began to infiltrate his speeches. Hackneyed political arguments, which we had hoped had been consigned to oblivion by the march of history, reappeared.

We were again told that during twenty years of Democratic Administrations there had been a dangerous 'usurpation of power by the Executive' and that this usurpation was responsible for whatever currently troubled us.

On the theory that the federal government was just another corporation written large, the Republican nominee promised to bring to high office men widely experienced in managing great industrial enterprises.

Everything henceforth would be done with business-like efficiency and decorum. A 'class-conscious' nation would be reunited, taxes would be reduced, the budget would be balanced, federal expenditures would be cut back, and, sooner or later, the Communists would be forced to sue for peace on American terms.

As the purchase price for the support of the stand-patters, General Eisenhower was persuaded to imply all this or to say it directly in the course of the 1952 Presidential campaign.

But once in office, President Eisenhower discovered that his initial compromises represented only a down payment on the continuing purchase price of Republican unity. In order to win Republican *Congressional* support additional concessions were demanded and given.

Yet the more the new President tried to conform to the

restrictive terms of the Republican party truce to which he had subscribed, the more difficult his position became as President.

Since it has been his avowed purpose to reduce the power of the Presidency, he could not logically act in the affirmative tradition of his immediate White House predecessors.

To do so would not only split his dearly purchased party unity, it would also smack of the very executive usurpation which he had been led to denounce so vigorously.

The stagnation of national leadership which resulted gave increasing leeway to the same backward-looking politicians who had bitterly opposed the Eisenhower nomination in 1952, and who had been made politically reckless and morally irresponsible by twenty years of impotent opposition to his predecessors.

In the Republican 83rd Congress, which the Eisenhower bandwagon narrowly swept into power, the committee chairmen promptly began to act as though they themselves had been elected President of the United States and as though Mr Eisenhower were the usurper. Republican spokesmen in Congress competed with one another in disrupting the whole process of orderly government.

Congressional investigations and individual Senators reached into the executive branch to dictate day-to-day policy on foreign affairs; to make a political football of the military establishment; to punish by adverse publicity those men who were guilty of no crime punishable by law; and to divide the President from his subordinates in the Administration.

Only when the control of Congress was returned to the Democrats after the 1954 elections was this unprecedented political extravaganza brought to an end.

Following his 1952 election victory, it is only fair to say that Mr Eisenhower made a genuine effort to identify the Republican party with liberal measures. From time to time, especially in advance of the 1956 elections, the White House supported modest programmes of public housing, slum clearance, Social Security, federal aid for school construction and increased minimum wages.

But the efforts of the more liberal wing were under constant pressures from the right wing. When the opportunity arose in 1959 to block an affirmative programme of liberal legislation by equating it with inflation, the Administration, with a year left in office, grasped it eagerly. Modern Republicanism thus came to an abrupt end.

Failing in its role as a socially minded government offering fresh and imaginative leadership, the Administration might still have made a valuable contribution to the streamlining of our federal government and to the improvement of its house-keeping.

After twenty years of innovation, there was, in fact, urgent need to tidy up our operations in any number of areas. There was also need for new standards of integrity among adminis-trators, for a consolidation of the military establishment, for reorganizing the White House, the postal service, the civil service, and so on.

Yet even when viewed solely as a housekeeping Administra-tion, appearing between a period of great economic and political ferment whose force was spent, and a similar new period struggling to be born, the Republican party's seven years of national leadership remains unimpressive.

With certain notable exceptions, its flood of businessmen and administrators have shown meagre understanding of the special demands of government. Moreover, by publicly pre-senting their services in the government as a generous but momentary interruption of their personal business affairs, they have revealed an unconscious lack of respect for the govern-mental process itself.

No sooner have many of them learned the mechanics of their new Washington assignment than they have submitted their letters of resignation to the President, citing their inability further to sacrifice their large corporate salaries for the modest compensation available in their country's service.

Moreover, standards of integrity are far short of what they should be. The Assistant to the President, the Secretary of the Air Force, and several others have left the government under a cloud of suspicion that they had used their high offices to promote their own business interests and those of their friends.

Meanwhile confusion within the military establishment has increased. Quarrelling at the Pentagon still defies all clear lines of responsibility. Inter-service rivalries for funds and programmes have been allowed to get so far out of hand that many responsible observers believe that the national security is threatened.

The White House has not been made into an effective instrument of executive action. The President has said he will wait until shortly before he leaves office to support a major White House reorganization so that no one will say that he himself will benefit.

The civil service and postal service have not been reorganized. In some places they have simply been eliminated.

Despite some conspicuous exceptions, the record of our most recent 'business-like' Administration in Washington has produced a new high in administrative confusion and managerial mediocrity.

The Republican party includes hundreds of thousands of liberal Americans who are deeply aware of the inadequacies which I have described, yet hopeful that a new Theodore Roosevelt, a Willkie or a Lincoln will come forward to lead us out of the political wilderness.

In the person of Governor Nelson Rockefeller of New York the Republicans have a figure who possesses a fine intelligence and broad human sympathies. I have known and respected Mr Rockefeller for years and I can attest to his distinguished personal merits.

Yet if Governor Rockefeller had been willing to run and

were to be elected President, America and the world would be treated to a twice-told political story. It would be the story of another good man raised to the Presidency by a spectacularly effective public relations effort, only to have the built-in conflicts of the Republican party itself hamstring or nullify almost everything creative or original that he might try to do at home or abroad.

CHAPTER XXVII

The Democratic Dilemma

THE Democrats will enter the 1960 campaign under their own special set of handicaps. These handicaps grow out of the nature of the party itself.

We have seen that much of the Democratic strength stems from two sources. First, it is a multi-interest party. Second, it is a national party, not only in name, but in its power to win major offices in all states of the Union.

Yet these two sources of strength transform themselves into dilemmas in the following ways. As a multi-interest party, the Democrats are often hard pressed to accommodate themselves to different and often antagonistic pressures.

So far they have managed to do this with exceptional skill. Witness the fact that they have elected a majority in both houses of Congress in twelve of the last fourteen Congressional elections.

Yet in the process of appealing to a wide variety of group interests, there is the very real danger that the overriding *national* interest may be lost sight of. This is so because the public interest is by no means the sum of all the individual interests to be found in the nation.

The authors of the federal Constitution saw this problem

clearly. They viewed the nation as a collective entity on a plane of its own, superior to all the parts which formed it.

If the Democratic party in an effort to cater to individual group pressures loses sight of this essential, it will fail adequately to serve the national interest and thereby weaken its appeal to the voters.

This is particularly so in an uneasy period like today when most Americans are weary of selfish scheming for special advantages and responsive to appeals in behalf of the greater public good.

The second dilemma of the Democrats is related to the first. It is that the Democratic party, from a desire to ease its internal differences and thereby maintain its unity as a national political party, may lose its integrity as a *liberal* party.

This dilemma was highlighted during the 1959 session of Congress. After it adjourned, many people were concerned by the failures of the overwhelming Democratic majority to assure the passage of more liberal legislation.

What these observers overlooked was the built-in power of the Presidency. This power is based on the prestige of the office itself, on the leverage of Presidential patronage, and on the traditional news dominance of the President himself over television and in the press.

In the Roosevelt era this combination enabled a liberal Administration to rally support for affirmative policies. In the hands of able conservatives, it has proved equally effective in blocking liberal legislation generated in Congress.

A contributing factor to the mixed record of Congress in 1959 lies in the disproportionate importance and seniority status of Democratic members from safe seats in the Deep South. When conservative Republicans and conservative Southern Democrats manoeuvre and vote together, as they often do on economic and civil rights issues, they may easily achieve a working majority.

The strength of the combination is illustrated by the vote on the original Landrum–Griffin labour reform bill which passed the House in August 1959. Ninety-six per cent of all House Democrats outside the eleven former Confederate states voted against this legislation. Yet when eighty-seven per cent of the Southern Democrats joined with eighty-nine per cent of the Republicans in supporting it, passage was assured.

Another example was provided by H.R. 3, a bill which Attorney General Rogers described as a dangerous and probably unconstitutional effort to undermine the authority of the Supreme Court. With one exception every Democratic member from the eleven former Confederate states voted for this legislation and in spite of the warning of the Republican Attorney General three out of every four Republicans joined them.

Although nine out of every ten non-Southern Democrats were opposed, the Southern–Republican combination again proved too strong.

No month goes by on Capitol Hill without similar examples of the often strange workings of our two-party system. And in each case the price paid by the Republicans has been the same : the continuing tacit agreement with the Southern bloc to sacrifice progress on civil rights for co-operation in blocking liberal economic legislation.

How does this add up? When we contrast the Northern Democrats and the Republicans we see two clearly defined political parties, the first overwhelmingly liberal in its orientation, and able to outvote its consistently conservative Republican opposition by a comfortable 4 to 3 majority.

But when the Southern Democrats join the Republicans, as they frequently do, the Democratic liberal forces lose by a ratio of roughly 6 to 5.

Some frustrated Northern liberals suggest that the problem can only be solved by writing off the Southern Democrats. They point out that F.D.R. and Harry Truman would have won five straight elections between them if every Southern electoral vote had been cast for their opponents.

Yet the suggestion that the Democrats should seek to achieve unity by the simple expedient of abandoning their position in the Southern states strikes me as irresponsible.

As a member of the 86th Congress I share the restlessness of many of my Northern, Eastern and Western associates with those conservative Southerners who vote as Republicans and then run for office as Democrats.

I am eager for a more vigorous attack on the problems at hand. I agree that compromise and delay often seem to have passed the point of practical necessity and relevance. I also agree that we should not repeat the Republican error of placing political unity above political principle.

Yet in our impatience let us not forget that the South has given the Democratic party and the nation some of its greatest liberal spirits – among them Jefferson, Jackson and Wilson.

In the 1930's such Southern leaders as Sam Rayburn of Texas, William B. Bankhead of Alabama, James F. Byrnes of South Carolina and Alben Barkley of Kentucky ushered Franklin D. Roosevelt's New Deal through Congress against bitter Republican opposition.

During World War II when the critically essential price, rent and wage control programme was under heavy fire, Southern Senators and Congressmen gave decisive support to the Office of Price Administration.

In the postwar period, when we were confronted with an unprecedented challenge overseas, Southern leaders took a leading role in support of the Truman–Marshall–Acheson–Vandenberg programme that helped keep Europe free.

From 1932 until about 1950 it may therefore be said that the Democratic party was basically united except on one issue – racial discrimination. Even here the differences, although deep, were obscured by Franklin D. Roosevelt's and Harry Truman's enormous personal popularity among Negro voters.

Through direct executive action these two Democratic

Presidents assured them equal status in the armed forces and indeed in all federal employment, and Negro voters are deeply grateful. As our most economically depressed group, Negroes also know that the Democratic party has been largely responsible for federal and state legislation to create better jobs, lower-cost housing and broader economic opportunities.

They understand that Republican leaders in Congress and, with relatively few exceptions, the Republican rank and file as well, have opposed such legislation. Moreover, in their efforts to block a liberal, expansionist economic progress Republican leaders have subscribed to the unspoken political deal to which I have referred that has consistently blocked civil rights legislation as well.

The voting coalition between conservative Republicans and conservative Democrats on economic matters has been highly effective in recent years. Yet the political price which the Republican party has paid to keep this coalition in smooth working order has been heavy and continuing.

At election time Republican candidates in the North have not hesitated to remind the Negro voter that theirs is the party of Lincoln. Yet with their election oratory and party platform safely behind them, they have felt forced – with some notable exceptions – to fulfil the terms of their economic alliance with Southern conservatives in bottling up, amending to death, or voting down legislation dealing with civil rights.

The Democratic party as a national party remains wide open to attack from a dedicated Republican liberal. But if he is to carry weight with the Negro voters he must persuade them that he is genuinely prepared to scrap his party's basic and functioning economic alliance with those Southern conservatives who still view the New Deal as alien socialism.

The situation is particularly complex because the forces which held most Southern Democrats to a liberal position on economic questions in the Roosevelt–Truman era have become weaker.

Southern industrialization has brought about an erosion of

the traditional free trade position of the Old South and a drift toward high tariffs and isolationism. It has also created a new group of conservative businessmen with great influence on many Southern political leaders.

As a result, Southern Democratic opposition to liberal economic legislative proposals has increased. This means that the incentives to maintain the tacit Republican–Southern Democratic alignment on civil rights have also increased.

In the meantime, the long-smouldering issue of segregation has been drawn into the political arena by white extremists following the Supreme Court decision of 1954. This will present the Democrats with a difficult challenge at their 1960 convention at Los Angeles.

The struggle of the Negro for equal status and opportunity is the current expression of our old American problem of digesting diverse human problems. Yet the nature and scope of the problem are changing dramatically.

As we approach the hundredth anniversary of the outbreak of the Civil War, half of all American Negroes are living in the North. There are now five times as many Negroes in Chicago as in Birmingham, four times as many in Detroit as in New Orleans, and six times as many in Los Angeles as in Miami.

Negro–white relationships have therefore ceased to be a sectional problem and are now a national one. Differences within the Democratic party can be eased only if the challenge is approached on that basis. This will require those Democrats who live outside the South not only to vote constructively in Congress but to face up to the need for more vigorous action in regard to discrimination in their own community backyards.

The record of much of the South on school desegregation has been distressingly slow. But when it comes to discrimination in housing and employment opportunities, so has the record of the North, East and West been slow.

During my term as Governor in 1949–51, Connecticut was the first state to desegregate its National Guard, to authorize a State Commission on Civil Rights, to prevent discrimination in all publicly owned housing, and to give a Fair Employment Practices Commission the power to prosecute offenders.

Ten years later only eleven out of thirty-nine non-Southern states have adopted antidiscrimination legislation affecting publicly assisted housing. Only four have such legislation affecting multi-unit private housing. Less than half have established Fair Employment Practices Commissions of any kind.

This means that most Northern states, some under Republican Administrations and some under Democratic, have thus far failed effectively to challenge the artificial walls which prevent the Negro from entering fully into their own community life as first-class citizens.

No Northern community that honestly examines its racial relations will deny that a substantial gap exists between the ideals its political leaders profess on election day and what they do in practice.

The Democratic party's dilemma can only be met by an honest, nationwide attack on the problem. As Democratic governors, mayors and legislators in Northern states and communities press for legislation that will assure the Negro an equal chance in employment and housing, more Southern Democrats may be encouraged to bring the same spirit to bear on their school segregation problem.

Most Southern political leaders insist that the situation there will take a long time to solve and that the Negro must be patient. No thoughtful man expects a quick solution.

The phrase 'with all deliberate speed', used in the Supreme Court decision, is in itself a clear recognition that the problem of school desegregation is shot through with complications that differ from place to place.

But it is now 183 years since a Southerner wrote the

Declaration of Independence, which declared the natural equality of *all* men – white and Negroes alike. And it is ninety-six years since the Emancipation Proclamation, which was meant to establish Negroes as free citizens of the Republic.

Is it any wonder that to American Negroes the word 'gradualism' has a hollow ring?

When the Supreme Court ruled that colour alone could no longer bar any child from a public school, most Americans were stirred deeply. Those who had long favoured desegregation thought the struggle had been won. Most of those who opposed it assumed that the only question now left unanswered was the timing and the technique.

With the judicial Rubicon crossed, the stage seemed set for constructive action. Yet progress generally has been slow. Why has this been true?

The law itself is a powerful teacher but the law touches only part of the problem. President Eisenhower said that his sole obligation was to enforce the law. He stressed that he had told no one, not even his wife, whether he thought the desegregation decision was right or wrong.

Thus, in resting on the oars of lawyers and judges, in saying that the question of desegregation was now purely a matter of law and order, the Administration has largely abdicated its broad responsibilities.

If this were merely a legal issue between those who believe in upholding the law and those who seek to circumvent it, there would have been no issue at all until the Supreme Court acted in 1954. Yet to argue this way is to turn the problem upside down.

The Court acted as it did because the Constitutional guarantee of equality involves the deepest *political* principles of this nation and because there was a *moral* issue presented which went to the heart of our Bill of Rights and of the Christian conscience.

It follows that the task of our political leaders, and of all who want to establish equal rights, is to look far beyond the mere enforcement of court decisions to the great human and moral questions that have thus far defied us. It is their task to convince the people that these decisions are not only legal but right.

This is no routine matter to be entrusted to the policeman on his beat. It calls for the rallying of our best and most authentic moral and political leadership – North, South, East and West.

As Senator Lyndon Johnson said : "Controversies involving civil rights have reached a point where they can be paralyzing to whole communities. But they are controversies which can be settled if the yawning chasm between people can be bridged . . . [by keeping] open the channels of communication among our people.'

With respect to all of this, the white Southerner has a case he can and should make. Generations of slavery, second-class Negro citizenship, inferior schools, houses and jobs have now returned to plague us with high rates of disease and crime and a low level of education in areas where Negroes predominate.

It is not too much to say that most American Negroes are suffering from the effects of a permanent depression. To correct this situation we must look well beyond the step-by-step integration of our schools.

If the Negro community is ill-housed, ill-fed, ill-clad; if it is sick, ignorant and angry, can the relatively comfortable whites be 'safe' in any realistic sense of the word?

As members of our one national political party, the lesson should be clear to Democratic leaders, South and North alike. There is no room any longer anywhere in America for low and inhuman standards of life for anyone of whatever colour.

The South's economic subservience to the industrial power of the North is now rapidly ending. Yet to gain the full benefits of its new industrialization, the South needs a capable labour force, trained in skills suited to the increasingly complex machines. It also needs prosperous consumers who have the means to buy the products of the new machines.

But so long as a major faction of its population is allowed to remain in a demoralized state, the new South will continue to deny this opportunity to itself.

Since the days of Thomas Jefferson, Southerners and Northerners have often marched together at the forefront of an advancing, progressive democracy as partners in a national Democratic party.

Today many Democratic Southerners in the House and the Senate are still sponsoring liberal measures to benefit the underprivileged throughout America.

John Sparkman and Albert Rains of Alabama are the most effective exponents of slum clearance and public housing. Lister Hill, also of Alabama, leads the fight for more adequate medical care.

Wright Patman of Texas and Albert Gore of Tennessee continue to speak out for an eased credit system as Andrew Jackson, the Populists and William Jennings Bryan did before them.

Yet it is the tragedy of many otherwise liberal Southerners that they have been compelled by local pressures to spend their creative energy fighting rearguard actions in defence of white supremacy principles which few of them personally believe in.

Has the time not come for a broad-gauged frontal assault on the social and economic problems which continue to hold the South in bondage?

From a political point of view, does the hope for a revitalized *national* liberal Democratic party not lie in the new industrial workers, the family farmers and the small businessmen who are certain to become an increasing political force in the new South?

On the issue of racial discrimination itself, legislation and court decisions will continue to be needed and they will continue to open up wounds. But does not the ultimate answer – North, South, East and West – lie in facing discrimination not as a legal question but as a challenge to our deepest moral convictions?

It is an abuse of language to talk about a 'Negro problem'. It is more precise to talk about a 'white problem' – the problem of the conscience of the Christian whites.

From the beginning of the Christian era it has been the Church's duty to preach the truth, even at the price of martyrdom. It was a white minister in the South, perhaps the most fervently religious section of our country, who said of the integration crisis : 'There's just one question to ask : What would Christ do?'

We know that Christ came to demonstrate the fatherhood of God and the brotherhood of man. We know we are our brother's keeper. Our religious and democratic faith tells us to get on with this most important task of our generation in every community and neighbourhood in America.

Only a cynic would suggest that we do this because two-thirds of the world is coloured and because our future security depends increasingly on their goodwill.

Nevertheless, it remains more true today than it was in 1947, when a distinguished former Secretary of State, Henry L. Stimson, wrote : 'No private programme and no public policy, in any section of our national life, can now escape from the compelling fact that if it is not framed with reference to the rest of the world it is framed with perfect futility.'

The quality of the Democratic response to the civil rights issue will determine whether the Democratic party, without substantial structural overhaul, will be able to or will deserve to achieve the political leadership of the fourth consensus. It is the testing question on which the soul of the party will be brought to judgment.

This is because the status of Negro citizens in our society, like our national capacity to expand economically and to conduct an effective foreign policy, is one of the master issues of our age. In it are caught up all the threads which connect foreign affairs with domestic legislation, economic advance with qualitative democracy, propaganda with action, ideals with deeds.

I am fully convinced that my party cannot legitimately lay claim to champion the Party of Hope unless it presses for a nation-wide solution, at once moral and workable, to this final phase of the struggle for equality in our society.

Whether the Democratic party will be able to lead our search for such a solution must in all frankness remain an open question. Certainly the obstacles are many and great. Perhaps my long and devoted association with the party has fathered unattainable wishes.

Yet I cannot help but believe that the Democratic party's history, traditions, structure and leadership provide it with the resources to surmount its internal obstacles, if it will summon the will and the vision to put these resources to work.

CHAPTER XXVIII

The Democratic Opportunity

THE Democratic party is not only the oldest political party in America, it is the oldest political party in the world. By and large, for 164 years it has provided the most effective political vehicle for those Americans who are most dedicated to the expansion of existing concepts of human dignity.

At times, it is true, the leadership of the Democratic party has drifted into the hands of men whose ideas were as firmly rooted in the *status quo* as were those of their opponents. Yet ultimately these leaders were submerged by liberal forces within their own ranks.

Thus the party, itself, has been able time and again to resume its vital role of redefining the American Dream within the framework of each generation's experience and needs, and thereby to assume the leadership of the Party of Hope.

Its original impetus came from Thomas Jefferson's crusade to limit the political power of the 'rich and well-born' and to place the destinies of the new Republic firmly in the hands of labourers, artisans, merchants and small farmers.

In the age of Andrew Jackson, this effort was broadened. Male suffrage was further extended, public education was encouraged, the open frontier was assured, and an effort made to break the power of the great private banking trusts that controlled not only the credit essential to the expansion of our economy but even our money supply.

Following the Presidencies of the two Jacksonians, Van Buren and Polk, the slavery issue split the Northern and Southern wings and the Democratic party lost most of its effectiveness.

In the 1870's it regained its vitality as the party of small farmers, tradesmen and the emerging new industrial labourers. In 1884 it elected a reform President in Grover Cleveland and, strengthened by a transfusion from the militant Populists of the Middle West and South, laid the foundation for Woodrow Wilson's New Freedom.

After the breath-catching and adjustment of the 1920's, the Democrats again rallied to provide the political vehicle with which Roosevelt and Truman created a new breakthrough of liberal thought and positive action in the 1930's and 1940's.

I do not disparage the historic work performed by great Republicans in the past. Their political heirs in the Republican party today continue to deserve our encouragement, despite their own discouragement.

But the greatest opportunity and the greatest penalties, if the opportunity is missed, now face the Democratic party.

As a national and multi-interest party, the Democrats will continue to confront troublesome internal differences and pressures. Yet I believe that one by one these questions will be resolved as others have been resolved in the past, and that the old alliance which Thomas Jefferson first put together will be reborn in a new framework for a new day and for new work.

The process of rebirth will itself become easier as the new consensus becomes more clearly expressed, as a new political leadership takes its place at the helm of the Democratic party, and as the newly enfranchised Negro and the newly recruited industrial worker in the South become more politically conscious.

This is not to suggest that the Democratic party will suddenly emerge as one happy liberal political family. On the contrary its internal debates are certain to continue in varying degrees of intensity.

Yet all this bickering serves a national as well as a party purpose. If the Democratic party did not exist as a great national shock absorber for clashing views, what would happen to the regular machinery of our government? Under pressure of conflicting interests, each with its own unyielding political apparatus, it might grind to a halt as the French Fourth Republic did.

What about the frequent charge in this connection that the Democrats are 'better politicians than the Republicans'?

Generally speaking, I believe this is the case. The Democrats are better politicians because the training they get within the framework of their multi-interest party better equips them to handle the intricate harmonizing process of our national government.

Democrats, moreover, are likely to take the business of government more seriously than do Republicans. They see government service not as a romantic interlude in a life devoted to personal affairs. They see it rather as a task demanding the best talents.

All this explains why I believe that the Democratic party, in spite of the differences between the majority wing in the North, East and West and the minority in the Deep South, is by all odds the best equipped to give form and content to the new political consensus now struggling to be born. In dealing with both domestic and foreign policy questions, its progressiveness, experience and traditional liberalism are decided advantages.

Take for example the conduct of foreign policy, which should be a central question in 1960. The liberal heritage of the Democratic party enables it to communicate with every people in every corner of today's upset world.

What could be more relevant to this critical election than the slogan 'The Rights of Man' which was used by the founders of the Democratic party in the 1796 Presidential campaign – the first in which they participated?

Those four simple words reflected an identity with the plain people of America and of the world. One hundred and sixty-four years later the plain people everywhere are still shouting them and in America the Democrats as a whole are still the most responsive.

The long close association of the Republican party leaders with the financial elite of America makes it difficult for them to understand the aspirations, insecurity and frustrations of the everyday people of Detroit, Seattle, Minneapolis or Sioux City.

How then can they be expected to understand the surging, conflicting reactions of those who live in New Delhi, Tokyo or Accra?

How can Republican economic planners who accept our present slow-paced rate of growth as normal appreciate the explosive impatience of Asian, African and Latin-American leaders attempting to ride the global revolutionary wave?

How can Republican party politicians – who still seek each year to hamstring the Tennessee Valley Authority and to block the Hell's Canyon project and who can rarely find room in their budgets for adequate unemployment compensation, schools, housing, hospitals and city planning – come to grips with the urgent development problems of the underdeveloped world?

How can the ideological descendants of those who denounced Jefferson, Jackson, Wilson and Roosevelt as radicals in their lifetime, reach out with sympathy and understanding to the new leaders of Asia, Africa and Latin America who know that the enduring principles for which Jefferson, Jackson, Wilson and F.D.R. stood are now the only alternatives to Communism?

Will the Democrats meet the challenge? Can the Democratic party provide the vehicle for the essential political breakthrough?

How the political record of 1960 is finally written will depend upon the choice of candidates, the choice of issues, and the dedication with which Democrats high and low approach the task at hand.

American voters have been fed a diet of expediency, timidity and courthouse politics, with a barrage of slogans thrown in, to becloud the challenge we face. They are now ready and waiting for a direct, straight-from-the-shoulder discussion of what needs to be done and how we can best proceed to do it.

The failures of the Republican party in domestic policy have been due to that party's inability to look beyond the special short-term interests which support it to create a framework for the *public* interest and to act within its context.

In dealing with foreign policy, Republican spokesmen have often appeared ready and eager to carry on their back assorted reactionaries around the globe.

It is essential that we Democrats advance a new and broader concept of the overriding *public* interest, both at home and overseas. This is so from whatever perspective we view ourselves, whether as a new government shaping a more affirmative foreign policy that will bring us closer to genuine peace, as an administration striving to create an economy of growing abundance without inflation, or as political leaders of a newly forming American consensus.

A resurgent Democratic party will insist that idle men, idle machines, and idle capital can no longer be allowed to exist side by side with unfulfilled public needs in housing, national defence, urban reconstruction, water resource development, school and hospital building and consumer goods.

It will oppose inflation, creeping or otherwise, and responsibly promote a rollback in prices.

It will seek practical answers to our fantastic agricultural dilemma in which food lies idle in storage at the taxpayers' expense while millions go hungry and farmers' incomes shrink.

It will denounce the special interests that seek to whittle away our natural resources for their own special benefit.

It will face racial discrimination for what it is : a national problem that exists to a greater or lesser degree in every community and which calls for *national* action that is moral as well as legal.

In foreign affairs a resurgent Democratic party, while insisting on adequate defences, will understand the long-term futility of a peace maintained only by mutual terror.

It will recognize the critical importance of a closely co-operating Atlantic Community and of a united Germany in a united Europe.

It will be conscious of the need to create free, friendly and more prosperous societies in Asia, Africa and Latin America.

In the language and tradition of Jefferson, Lincoln, Wilson and Roosevelt, it will associate itself responsibly with the continuing anti-colonial revolution for human dignity.

In other words, a Democratic party worthy of its great past will understand the sweep and promise of the American liberal tradition and the pressing need to refocus that tradition on the problems of today's explosive yet infinitely promising world.

History has once again placed a mighty challenge before the Democratic party. Its task in the decisive year of 1960 is to break through the mists of memory and to reassert, for our day and age, its claim to leadership of the Party of Hope.